Personal Safety and Security Playbook

T0348843

Personal Safety and Security Playbook

Risk Mitigation Guidance for Individuals, Families, Organizations, and Communities

Francis J. D'Addario

ELSEVIER

AMSTERDAM • BOSTON • HEIDELBERG • LONDON
NEW YORK • OXFORD • PARIS • SAN DIEGO
SAN FRANCISCO • SINGAPORE • SYDNEY • TOKYO

Security
Executive Council

Elsevier
The Boulevard, Langford Lane, Kidlington, Oxford, OX5 1GB, UK
225 Wyman Street, Waltham, MA 02451, USA

Originally published by the Security Executive Council, 2009

Notices
Knowledge and best practice in this field are constantly changing. As new research
and experience broaden our understanding, changes in research methods,
professional practices, or medical treatment may become necessary.

Practitioners and researchers must always rely on their own experience and knowledge
in evaluating and using any information, methods, compounds, or experiments
described herein. In using such information or methods they should be mindful of their
own safety and the safety of others, including parties for whom they have a professional
responsibility.

To the fullest extent of the law, neither the Publisher nor the authors, contributors,
or editors, assume any liability for any injury and/or damage to persons or property
as a matter of products liability, negligence or otherwise, or from any use or operation
of any methods, products, instructions, or ideas contained in the material herein.

British Library Cataloguing-in-Publication Data
A catalogue record for this book is available from the British Library

Library of Congress Cataloging-in-Publication Data
A catalog record for this book is available from the Library of Congress

ISBN: 978-0-12-417226-5

This book has been manufactured using Print On Demand technology. Each copy
is produced to order and is limited to black ink. The online version of this book
will show color figures where appropriate.

Working together
to grow libraries in
developing countries

www.elsevier.com • www.bookaid.org

CONTENTS

EXECUTIVE SUMMARY

Reducing or mitigating personal safety and security risk is a priority concern for individuals, families, organizations, and communities. The *Personal Safety and Security Playbook* is designed for anyone who may benefit from shared community safety and security responsibilities. The guidance in this playbook covers personal safety and security concerns and risks both on and off the job. It may be used prior to a problem arising, or as a reference and resource during a security situation.

In any organization, personal safety and security are shared responsibilities. Messaging our intentions is only a first step. Our brand, community, and individual reputations depend on risk awareness, reporting, response, and mitigation performance. With that in mind, the purpose of the *Personal Safety and Security Playbook* is to serve as a reminder to always put people first. The chapters in this playbook are organized by areas of concern, such as personal protection and safety, protecting children, protecting your home, being secure at work, and much more.

WHAT IS A PLAYBOOK?

A playbook is an excellent tool for the security or business leader who wants to develop, implement, enhance, or validate a specific aspect of a security or risk management program. Playbooks provide a detailed treatment of a security program or service that can be quickly and effectively applied to an immediate need within an organization. Playbooks define and present the essential elements most often used by successful practitioners. They provide a framework that a security professional can use to set up, manage, and communicate the program to stakeholders. They can also be used by non-security personnel who need an introduction and plan for action on a new security-related job responsibility. Playbooks are particularly useful for educators that are committed to providing current, relevant information and practices distilled from successful practitioners and programs and that have a direct correlation to current security position.

INTRODUCTION

Our collective security and safety relies on many variables, including our self-awareness and that of others. Family member, neighbor, co-worker, public safety professional, and subject matter expert participation is necessary for personal security. Timely situational risk recognition and communications before, during, and after threatening events can significantly improve outcomes including injury and loss.

The guidelines in this playbook are designed to be a reference for issues concerning your personal security. They cover a wide range of topics, from personal risk awareness to protection and security considerations for family, home, travel, and work.

There are many agencies and resources that can help you improve your security and that of your family and community. In this playbook, we encourage you to become your own resource. To be diligent. To rely on your own instincts and intuition. To responsibly report persons and situations that make you afraid for your co-workers, family, neighbors, or yourself. And to seek advice and assistance from trusted professionals.

There is no one document that can be taken off the shelf to perfectly inform personal safety and security. Ultimately, you must assess your particular risks and make your own safety and security choices. Timely communication of "need to know" hazards to public safety and private professional resources is key to managing consequences.

Be safe. Be secure.

***

Special thanks goes to the National Crime Prevention Council for use of many of their materials in developing this playbook.

CHAPTER 1

Preventing and Reporting High-Risk Events

1.1 OVERVIEW

As you consider the issues of personal security, remember that there are three important things you need do to: 1. Look out for yourself, your family, neighbors and colleagues; 2. Be engaged at home and at work and with volunteer organizations; and 3. Get involved in your community.

- Understand and watch for early signs of risk (those situations or conditions that concern you or make you afraid for the safety or security of others).
- Take steps to reduce the likelihood of becoming a victim.
- Work with resources on the job and off including neighborhood groups to make your surroundings safe and secure.
- Report crimes and hazards immediately and cooperate with responding or investigating agencies.
- Provide support to people who have been victimized.
- Actively promote awareness.

1.2 CRIME PREVENTION AND HAZARD MITIGATION

You have the right to live a secure and comfortable life, free from the fear of crime, violence and other situational risks. Unfortunately, whether you are at home, on vacation, or at work, threats and hazards are all around. You can significantly reduce the risk to yourself and others by following some common-sense tips and taking direct actions.

There are many ways to prevent crime or mitigate hazardous conditions, and each circumstance may require a specific response. Personal security and safety begins by knowing the basics of prevention:

- Reduce the opportunities for crime and accidents.
- Familiarize yourself with locally relevant hazards alerts, emergency reporting and preparedness guidelines.
- Public safety organizations including police and fire departments are typically excellent resources.
- Work with your employer, public safety and volunteer neighborhood organizations.
- Design an environment that fosters a sense of community.
- Watch for early signs of problems and take action when you see them.
- Actively promote awareness of the issues.
- Ensure communications options awareness and availability

1.2.1 Reduce the Opportunities for Crime and Accidents

Risk reduction opportunities depend on people taking a proactive stance toward personal safety and security. Be knowledgeable, equipped and trained.

- Be sure that your family knows accident, crime and fire prevention basics. Self-protection skills, how to react in an emergency and CPR or first aid techniques are valuable. Be aware of the issues.
- Ensure fire extinguishers, smoke alarm batteries, generator fuel, emergency supplies including food and water, contact lists and your emergency plan are proactively checked and refreshed for readiness.
- Store weapons and combustible materials securely in approved safety containers.
- Install consumer rated protective equipment including locking, lighting and detection devices.
- Know where your children or dependent seniors are and know what they are doing.

- Avoid leaving them unsupervised or supervised by a person who has not undergone a diligence investigation or you do not implicitly trust.
- Family members and caregivers should be briefed on household security and emergency preparedness plans including communications and rendezvous meeting places. Practice your plan. Training from a certified agency for neighborhood groups may be ideal.
- Walk, jog or hike with companion(s) in well lit, public safety patrolled areas against traffic with communications capability. Carry a mobile phone. Share your itinerary for more remote destinations. Check in with others on departure and arrival.
- Know the risk of travel destinations. Ensure the use of seatbelts, hands-free communications, GPS assistance and emergency supplies in any family vehicle. Consider roadside assistance.
- Report crimes, hazardous conditions (accidents, crimes, smoke, fire etc.) and suspicious behavior immediately to public safety agencies when it is safe to do so.
- Consider Crime stoppers and anonymous reporting ethics lines if you feel afraid to step forward as a witness for serious crimes.
- Find ways to resolve conflict nonviolently. The regular use of common courtesy and good manners helps to keep arguments from ending in violence. Involve supervisors and need-to-know subject matter experts when you feel afraid.

1.2.2 Work with Your Neighborhood Organizations
Get involved. Volunteer to help in community and neighborhood anti-crime and safety programs such as Neighborhood Watch, McGruff House, or other sanctioned public safety organizations.

- If you cannot find a group that already exists in your neighborhood, start one. Federal, provincial, county or city public safety referral agencies are generally excellent resources.
- Encourage participation of groups that already have a stake in neighborhood safety local businesses, tenants' or homeowners' associations, churches, and fraternal or social organizations.
- Partner with local public safety officials for voluntary background diligence. (Don't assume that community volunteers will not be predators).
- Look for training and certification.

- Consider all local man-made and natural environmental hazards. If you are in a hurricane, seismic, tornado, or wildfire prone area, volunteers for all-hazards are prized by first responder organizations who may need assistance ranging from crime prevention to search and rescue operations.

1.2.3 Design an Environment that Fosters a Sense of Community

Many communities are working with their neighborhood associations to make themselves attractive. Changing the environment from one that promotes isolation and fear to one that brings out the best in people is ideal. This involves messaging community care. Think about attracting good good neighbors and deterring others.

- Communities that present a unified front against crime can deter criminals from gaining a foothold. They can also expedite detection and response to other hazards like accidents, fires and manmade or natural disasters. When a community's residents feel that they have a stake in a better future, they are more likely to take unified and proactive action.
- Local public safety agencies have staff members who can help you prevent and mitigate accidents, crimes, fires and unwanted outcomes from other environmental risks. There are also municipal, county, provincial, state and federal offices that assist crime prevention and disaster preparedness and assistance efforts.
- Involve teens, seniors, and children in ridding the neighborhood of litter and graffiti.
- Contact the public works department for help or expert guidance when cleaning up your neighborhood. Removal of hazardous materials including chemicals, debris, materials (asbestos) sharps (hypodermic needles) and solvents may require technical assistance.
- Volunteer your home as a safe haven or watch-house for schoolbus riders or children who are scared or need assistance. Make certain the volunteer organization is vetted and approved by local public safety agencies.
- Hold block meetings and discuss specific ways to fight crime or be better prepared for emergencies. Get to know your neighbors and agree to look out for each other.

1.2.4 Watch for Early Signs of Problems

As you walk or drive through your neighborhood, pay attention to your instincts. Small items often can alert you to bigger problems. Early warning signs may be the first clue that personal security and safety issues are getting larger.

- Abandoned buildings and vehicles, graffiti, litter, loitering, and vandalism may signal more serious issues.
- Be alert and request public agency assistance for more overt signs of growing problems. Reported accidents, crimes and first responder calls are part of the local public record if not reported by responsible newspapers or blogs. Serious crime trends, like arsons, assaults, drug trafficking, injury accidents, kidnapping, and robberies should be of particular concern.
- Crimes are routinely reported by address and zipcode by many police agencies on their public-facing internet sites. Additional patrols, detection technologies and other resources may be required and requested to reverse troubling conditions.

1.2.5 Actively Promote Awareness of Personal Security and Safety Issues

One of the most important ways to increase your personal security and the security of those around you is to promote awareness of personal security issues:

- Talk to family and neighbors about local risks and resources.
- Teach your children to communicate their plans, whereabouts and companion destinations. Check-in and status reporting works well as a model expectation.
- Train for risk avoidance, mitigation and self-protection skills including emergency preparedness, first aid, or lifeguarding. Automated external defibrillator (AED) training is also available as those devices for cardiac arrest are more commonly provided in work and public community spaces. Model proven behaviors.
- Adopt routine location and status communications. Establish household and public emergency rendezvous points.
- Advocate nonviolent solutions for conflict
- Support neighborhood and workplace crime prevention and safety programs.

- Encourage family members to learn sexual assault prevention strategies.
- Get involved with making schools safer.

1.3 CONFLICT MANAGEMENT

Frustrated that your neighbor will not clean up his backyard? Angry because a driver cuts in front of you? Irritated with someone at work? Conflict is part of life—creating stress, hurting friendships, and even causing injury or death.

Learning how to manage conflict improves the quality of our lives, our relationships with others, and our productivity at work. Conflict is a legitimate and important process that people can learn to manage, often by developing proactive communication and conflict management skills.

1.3.1 Be Aware of the Causes and Patterns of Conflict
The first step in managing conflict is to become aware of the causes and patterns of conflict in your life.

- Identify how others can trigger an emotional response in you. Is it by means of a facial expression, a tone of voice, or a certain phrase?
- If a colleague, family member, a friend, or a neighbor is making you angry, let him or her know. Small problems that are not addressed can grow into big problems.
- Recognize what specific situations, such as rush hour traffic, usually cause stress and conflict.
- Look at the way you usually handle stress. Is it working? If not, you may want to try something new, such as learning to be a better listener.

1.3.2 Understand the Other Person's Point of View
- During an argument, do not concentrate on what you are going to say next. Instead, listen to what the other person is saying. Go beyond the words and try to understand the feelings of the other person.
- Show that you are listening to the other person through your facial expression and body language.
- Step back from the problem. Try to get the facts straight. Brainstorm all the ideas that might resolve the argument.
- Check for understanding.

- Indicate that you are willing to find a solution.
- Find something that you can agree on.

1.3.3 Reaching an Agreement
There are a few basic principles to follow when trying to reach agreement in situations that involve stress:

- Talk about the issues without insulting or blaming the other person.
- Avoid stating your position. Try to talk about the problem objectively.
- Together, discuss new ways of solving the problem. Be open to innovation and new ideas.
- If you come to an agreement, make sure both of you understand who will be responsible for follow-through and specific actions.

1.3.4 If You Cannot Reach an Agreement, Get Help
Sometimes you will not be able to reach agreement. You may want to seek an outside party to help resolve the situation. Local government, private organizations, and colleges offer a broad range of arbitration and mediation services. See the next section, *Mediation and Negotiation*.

1.4 MEDIATION AND NEGOTIATION

Sometimes a conflict is too difficult for you to resolve on your own. Just as there is no one cause for conflict, there is no one means of resolution. The important thing to remember is to keep trying and remain determined to find a solution to the problem. Rare exceptions include those situations where you are specifically threatened or feel afraid. Those situations may be best resolved by reporting intimidation to "need to know" organizational security or public safety agencies.

More and more often, professional mediators, arbitrators, and ombudsmen are helping people resolve conflict, relieving the backlog in overburdened courts. Neighborhood organizations, local governments, law schools, the Better Business Bureau, as well as private organizations, all offer mediation and arbitration services.

- *Mediators* are unbiased and detached from the problem. They do not dictate a settlement but help you find a solution by defining areas of agreement/disagreement, encouraging discussion, and providing guidance. Mediation sessions are confidential.

- *Arbitrators* act like judges in a dispute. Arbitrators are chosen by both parties. They hear evidence from both sides and then hand down a decision, which is usually final. Sometimes a panel of arbitrators decide by majority vote the outcome of a complaint.
- *Ombudsmen* are used by institutions or government agencies to recommend that certain policies or practices should be changed. Legislatures, health care agencies, and educational systems frequently appoint ombudsmen to investigate complaints from the public and to resolve problems.

For more detailed information, consult trusted advisors or search the internet and/or local directories for reputable, Better Business or consumer rated arbitration or mediation services.

Information may also be obtained from:

National Institute for Advanced Conflict Resolution
http://www.niacr.org/
National Association for Mediation in Education
http://www.servicelearning.org/library/lib_cat/index.php?
library_id = 697
(866) 245-SERV (7378)
Community Boards Program
http://www.communityboards.org/
(415) 920-3820
National Crime Prevention Council
http://www.ncpc.org/
(202) 466-6272

1.5 REPORTING CRIMES AND EMERGENCIES

With more than 5 million deaths every year, violence and injuries account for 9 percent of global mortality, as many deaths as from HIV, malaria, and tuberculosis combined. Eight of the 15 leading causes of death for people ages 15 to 29 years are injury-related: road traffic injuries, suicides, homicides, drownings, burns, war injuries, poisonings, and falls.[1]

Every 25 seconds, a violent crime such as a murder, rape, robbery, or assault is reported to police somewhere in the United States.

[1]"10 Facts on Injuries and Violence," World Health Organization, http://www.who.int/features/factfiles/injuries/en/index.html.

However, fewer than half of all the violent crimes that are committed actually get reported.

Criminals whose actions go unreported continue to inflict pain, violence, and loss upon their victims. Reporting crimes is one of the best ways to protect yourself and your children and to prevent new crimes from occurring. More and more, communities are banding together through neighborhood watches and patrols in a clear show of solidarity against violent crime.

Data routinely indicates that timely reporting of accidents, crimes, fires and medical emergencies enables better outcomes for victims when trained responders arrive on the scene quicker. For instance, heart attack victims lose 10% of their survivability with each minute. Injury and property outcomes also diminish with passing seconds of an undetected, unreported or unsuppressed fire.

Consider roadside assistance services that feature emergency response assistance.

Taking greater responsibility for reporting any risk event, hazardous condition or emergency is the first step in creating safer communities in which to live and work:

- Know what kinds of incidents to report.
- Know how to report the facts associated with crimes and suspicious activity.
- Protect yourself when reporting crimes.

1.5.1 What Kinds of Incidents to Report
- Someone screaming or shouting for help
- Building or superstructure collapse, smoke or fire
- Unusual noises like explosions, gunshots and glass breaks
- Serious accidents, severe weather impacts (treefalls on homes) and conditions like downed power lines
- Crimes in progress including assaults, burglaries, or robberies
- Suspicious persons and vehicles at school bus stops, playgrounds, parking lots or in a neighbor's yard or driveway when they are vacation
- Cars, vans, or trucks driving recklessly or suspiciously slow, without lights after dark

- Anyone being forced into a vehicle
- A stranger sitting in vehicle or stopping a vehicle to talk to a child
- Abandoned vehicles or property
- Any situation that makes you intuitively afraid for your own safety or that of others

1.5.2 How to Report a Crime, Suspicious Activity, or Emergency

- First, get the facts. Make note of, video, or photograph license plate numbers, suspicious persons, or vehicles if it is safe to do so.
- Determine your location to aid responders: address, floor, unit number, milemarker, or adjacency to landmarks, businesses, schools. (Note that low cost security and safety apps are available for smartphone users. They allow automatic connectivity to public safety responders and communicate your GPS location even when you are on the move or fleeing a risk situation.)
- When you call on-site security law enforcement, provide your name and address if you feel you are not at risk to do so.
- Describe the event (what happened, when, where, and who was involved).
- Describe the suspect(s) (sex and race, age, height, weight, hair color, clothing, hat or footwear descriptions including colors, patterns, and logos, and personal distinctive characteristics such as facial hair, scars, tattoos, or accents).
- If a vehicle was involved, describe it in detail (color, make, model, year, license plate, and any special features such as stickers, dents, or decals).
- Note anything a suspect may have touched or left behind for police investigative interest.
- Let injured victims know help is on the way. Render first aid or CPR if you are competently trained and it is safe to do so.

1.5.3 Protect Yourself When Reporting Crimes
It is sometimes best to remain anonymous when reporting a crime.

- Although it is important to provide investigators with contact information, in case they need to contact you, you have the right to request that your personal identity be withheld from the general public. Consider offering an e-mail or messaging number rather than a home phone and address.
- If you are a witness testifying in court, you typically do not have to provide your home or work address in the courtroom.

- In the United States and other western countries your employer may not discipline or dismiss you for testifying in court.
- Request victim assistance or witness assistance from responding agencies.

1.6 VICTIM'S ASSISTANCE AND RIGHTS

Many federal goverments, states, provinces, counties, or cities have agency offices for victim's assistance. Agencies and non-governmental organizations render aid or offer assistance to victims of catastrophic accidents, crime and natural disasters. Those who require application assistance, suspect their rights have been violated, feel that they have been treated unfairly, or need assistance with mediation or other services should make inquiries.

Contact your relevant local department of public safety to ask for the contact information regarding victim's assistance or rights office that serves your area.

You may find some or all of the following rights to be part of the victim's rights provisions or laws.

- Notification of important benefits, registration requirements, and proceedings and protections that they may elect to participate in
- Protection from further harm
- Financial assistance or restitution
- Medical or psychological assistance

Witnesses often have the same rights, except for the right to receive financial help.

1.6.1 Notification of Events and Rights

Victims and witness usually have the right to be notified of their rights, of any plea agreements, parole hearings, and probation/parole statuses; changes in court schedules, dates, times, and places of sentencing; and the offender's release from prison or another institution. These provisions are not always part of state law, so contact your state's attorney general's office to find out about your rights as a victim or witness.

1.6.2 Participation in Prosecution

Victims typically have the right to participate in prosecution, including the right to:

- Inform the court of the impact of the crime at both pre-trial hearings and sentencing;
- Object to any plea bargaining arrangement;
- Request a speedy trial;
- Bring a supportive person with them to pre-trial hearings;
- Attend sentencing; and
- Give written objections to sentencing.

1.6.3 Special Protections
Victims and witnesses have the right to certain special protections.

- Tampering with a witness is against the law.
- Witnesses do not have to provide their home or work address in court.
- Employers may not discipline or dismiss victims or witnesses who are called to testify in court.

Victims may also be eligible for financial assistance if they have suffered economic loss. They may request of the court that restitution be paid.

1.7 USING AVAILABLE RESOURCES

A vast array of resources is available to help you enhance personal security and safety as you mitigate risk for yourself, your family, your colleagues, and your community.

These resources include those referred to here, as well as others offered by international NGOs, federal, provincial and state public safety, emergency preparedness and other agencies. Be inquisitive. Search the World Wide Web and agency sites for current advice and guidelines. Consult internal advisors as well as those who represent reputable national, regional, local and neighborhood organizations, publications, for endorsed subject matter expert documentation.

Information about these resources is summarized in Chapter 14: Personal Security Resources. As you read that chapter, if you do not find what you are looking for, or if you have a question, contact your local county, municipal, provincial, state, or federal public safety agencies.

CHAPTER 2

Personal Protection

2.1 OVERVIEW

Personal protection involves taking personal responsibility for the security safety of yourself and those close to you. All personal protection methods are built on four fundamental concepts:

1. Be prepared.
2. Stay alert to your surroundings.
3. Take steps to reduce the chance that you will become a victim.
4. Plan and acquire the wherewithal to mitigate consequences if you are at risk, or are victimized by an accident, a crime or natural disaster.

This chapter provides information on ways to protect yourself in a wide variety of settings and situations (at home, when you are driving, when you are at work, and many others).

Chapter 3: Assault and Sexual Assault provides personal security information for situations that involve violence.

2.2 AT HOME

This section has a few tips for helping you be more secure and safe in your home. For more detailed information about home security, see Chapter 5: Home Safety and Security.

- Before you buy or rent, request the local crime reporting for your neighborhood. Severe weather and seismic risks are fairly well mapped and, along with school district and public safety agency reputations, may inform your decisions.
- The most vulnerable points of entry into your house are doors and windows. Be certain that you secure all the doors to the outside with dead bolt locks. Always lock your doors and windows, even when you are at home. Secure extra keys out of sight and remove house keys or access control fobs for your residence from the ring when using automobile or valet services.
- Ensure that hardware, including locks, door striking plates, smoke, radon or carbon monoxide detectors are properly installed. Fire extinguisher, first aid, and emergency preparedness supplies should be thoughtfully located.
- If you have a deadly or non-lethal weapon seek professional training. Secure weapons as prescribed by law and ensure they are not accessible by children. Cypher lock boxes enable instant access while providing needed security.
- Use a peephole or other viewer to see who is at the door before you let someone into your home. Make certain delivery personnel are uniformed and accompanied by a well marked vehicle that identifies the organization.
- Consider investing in a monitored home alarm system that may detect and record intrusion, smoke or fire, the presence of debilitating gas or other hazardous conditions.
- If you are home alone, do not let a person at the door or on the phone know it. Use phrases like "We are not interested" or "We cannot talk now" to indicate that someone else is with you.
- Do not let a service person enter your home without checking professional credentials. Since it is difficult to determine whether

credentials are valid, it is best to deny entrance to anyone who does not have an appointment.

- Do not let strangers in to use the phone. In an emergency, offer to place a call yourself or direct the person to a pay phone.
- If you receive a number of harassing or obscene calls, note the origination number, time, date and content of the conversation. Contact the telephone company security, request an investigation and make a police report. Consider caller identification or other recommendations by the subject matter experts.
- Keep emergency numbers near your phone. Include your address for babysitters. Teach children how to use the telephone to make 911 or other public safety calls.
- Teach children the right way to answer the door and the telephone. They should not give out information about who is home, who is out, or how long they will be gone. "My mom or dad can't talk right now, may I take a message?"
- If your children spend time alone at home, take the necessary precautions. See the topic *Home Alone: Latchkey Children* in Chapter 4: Children for more information.
- Use only your last name and first initial on your mailbox and in your telephone listing.
- Do not attach your home address to your key chain. Consider an email or work address for your key chain. This may help the return of lost keys without informing a stranger where you live.
- If you do lose your keys and wallet or personal address identification, consider changing your locks immediately.
- Use motion detector security lights to increase the lighting in dark areas around your home, especially around windows and doors. They will alert you for visitors and enable just in time lighting assistance to prevent trips and falls while controlling utility expenditure.
- Do not provide hiding places (such as bushes and trees) near your windows and doors. All shrubs and bushes around your door and windows should be kept trimmed. Cacti, thorny roses and berry bushes may offer homeowner benefits while presenting a more deterrant perimeter for trespassers.
- Keep your windows covered so that your activities are private.
- Designate an interior safe room(s) with deadbolt protecton, security hardened door hardware, wall reinforcement and communications for additional intruder protection.

- Designate an interior or basement saferoom for severe weather or other natural disasters. Store emergency provisions including food, water, radio, flashlights, batteries and first aid supplies and mobile charger. Consider a generator to support lights, chargers, a safety rated portable heater and perishable refrigeration.
- Keep a working sound device or an alarm-company-monitored panic button near your bed on your key chain and in other parts of your home. A loud sounder, such as a siren, may be effective in frightening away an intruder or alerting neighbors to an emergency.
- Explore insurance discounts for home, vehicle security and alarm systems.

2.3 DOMESTIC VIOLENCE

Domestic violence can happen in homes where you would not expect it. It can destroy families, ruin careers, and end lives unless action is taken.

2.3.1 If Someone You Know Is Involved in Domestic Violence

Domestic violence is often a hidden crime because victims are afraid or ashamed to come forward.

If you feel that someone you know may be involved in a violent domestic situation, stay alert to the signs of abuse.

- Signs of abuse may include accusations of unfaithfulness or infidelity, attempts to humiliate someone in public, efforts to control financial resources, destruction of personal property, persistent "accidental" injuries or incidents of physical or verbal threats.
- If you know someone who is living with domestic violence, provide support. Encourage the person to seek professional assistance. Be patient and understanding.

2.3.2 If You Are the Victim of Abuse

Ignoring the problems relating to domestic violence may make them worse.

- If you are a victim of abuse, contact local victims assistance agencies and the police to report the assault. Local agencies often offer a range of advice and resources including safe havens for those at risk.

- Get medical attention immediately. Ask the doctor or emergency room staff to photograph your injuries.
- Secrecy increases the abuser's power over you. Break the silence. Talk to a friend or neighbor, a need to know supervisor or call a domestic violence hotline.
- Leave your home immediately if you feel you or your children are in danger.
- Have a plan of action to prepare for the next attack. If you cannot be found at home you may be stalked at work or a family member's house. Know where you will go and set aside some money.
- Ask a professional about recommended protection options including bringing a criminal complaint and seeking a civil protection order.

2.3.3 If You Have Hurt Someone

Physical assault is against the law. Leaving the scene of an accident with injuries or willful battery of others can have irreparable civil, criminal, employment, family and social consequences.

- Seek counseling if you have hurt anyone in your family. Confidential help is often available under subsidized employee assistance plans or private and public agencies. Learn constructive ways to work out your tension and anger, such as taking a walk or playing sports. Avoid alcohol or illegal drugs, which can only make the problem worse.
- End the cycle of abuse. If you resort to violence to settle arguments, that is what you will teach your children. Help kids to respect themselves and consider the feelings of others.

For more information about how victims can receive help and how perpetrators can receive counseling, contact your local public health and safety agencies or search the web for domestic violence services in your city, county, province or state.

2.4 OBSCENE, THREATENING, HARASSING, AND INAPPROPRIATE COMMUNICATIONS

Handling inappropriate attention, phone calls, e-mails and messages at home with a clear sense of what to do is important both for your protection and helping public safety agencies in identifying the suspect.

See Chapter 6: Workplace Safety and Security for more information about handling inappropriate phone calls at work.

Unknown and known communicators can inappropriately contact you by phone, email or other means to harass or victimize you. They may also can attempt to collect information that might help them access an account, steal your identity or burglarize your residence. Attempts to collect information from victims at home can occur anytime.

If you receive obscene, suspicious or threatening communications:

- Discontinue the conversation immediately if you feel afraid.
- Refrain from providing personal information, dates of birth, address information, account or password information unless you are communicating with a trusted service provider that you have contacted.
- Be aware of social engineering and phishing scams that take place on personal computer and mobile device networks. Criminals often lure unsuspecting victims to click a link for security alerts or other fraudulent offers.
- Pedophiles and other criminals pose as children on the internet or otherwise misrepresent themselves by telephone to lure children and unsuspecting adults into disclosing information or meeting them with unforeseen consequences.
- Report threats or harassment and inappropriate communications via the internet, telephone, or mobile service providers and/or police immediately. Most communication and service companies and agencies have web-listed resources for fraud, harassment or security service assistance.
- For inapproriate telephone communications, ask for call trace, caller identification or blocking assistance. Be certain to report all other suspicious calls that seem to be related. Keep a notepad available for dates, times, and exact content of calls.
- If the call or contact is stored as a message on email account, your answering machine or voice mail, do not erase it. It may be consequential evidence for investigators.
- If the number is captured by a caller ID system, do not erase the number.

2.4.1 If You Talk Directly to the Caller
Your memory may be the only record of an obscene or harassing call. Try to listen for information that can help police establish the caller's

identity. Advise the caller to cease and desist and that you are reporting the incident. Note details including time and date immediately.

- If you know the caller's identity, write it down. Write down the time the person called and what he or she said.
- Age and gender: Is the caller young or old, male or female?
- Tone of voice and manner: Is the caller excited or calm, rational or irrational, deliberate or confused?
- Familiarity: Is the caller's voice familiar? Does he or she have an accent? Did the voice sound disguised? Did the caller seem to know your schedule or any other information about you?
- Background noise: Is there any background noise that would help to pinpoint the location of the call? For example, any office equipment or factory machinery? Sounds that suggest a public pay telephone? A public address system? Static on the line? Bus, train or airport announcements?
- Do calls appear to be random or are they coincidental to your arriving or leaving your home, job, recreational or volunteer activities etc.?
- Any detectable pattern or nuance is helpful for investigators.
- Harassment on the job should be reported to need to know supervisors and site security personnel.

2.5 STALKING BEHAVIOR

Stalking is a form of harassment. Stalkers want to manipulate you and control you. The way you respond to a stalker could encourage the behavior.

Stalking is usually performed by someone who knows the person being stalked. The harassment target is often a current or former co-worker, neighbor, spouse, or lover. The target person is typically an unreciprocating infatuation or someone perceived to have committed some wrong.

- If you believe you are being stalked, contact your local public safety agency for guidance. If you are being stalked while at work, let your manager or immediate supervisor know immediately. Seek advice for criminal complaints or civil restraining orders.
- Be prepared to provide a complete description of the suspect. Include a chronological history of events, sighting or contact details,

the time(s) and date(s) that you may have communicated a cease and desist request; as well as any known witness and suspect vehicle details.

- Gifts, notes, voicemail and all unwanted attention evidence should be chronologically recorded by date and time and saved, witnessed, photographed and stored for investigative examination.
- Actively look for your antagonist in your neighborhood or around your employment. If you have a photograph or description, share it with co-workers and neighbors. Make extra turns when leaving your employment or residence to acsertain if you are being followed. Keep your mobile telephone in your hand when walking or in a hands free when driving to report being followed.
- Know the whereabouts of your family members. Family members can also become targets.
- Consider delisting phone numbers and address information or removing them from your personal checks and business cards.
- Use a private mailbox service or postal box to receive your personal mail.
- Report every occurrence of the stalker's contact attempts or presence to site security or public safety investigators.
- Consider joining a support group or seeking professional consultation.
- Explore self defense training options, alarming your home and vehicle, and roadside emergency assistance.
- Determine insurance discounts for proactive protection investments.

2.6 IF YOU LIVE IN A RURAL SETTING

Rural communities have their own unique problems, such as theft of crops, livestock, and equipment. Although such crimes as burglary, rape, assault, and auto theft occur with less frequency in rural areas, they still occur. In addition, rural youth have the same problems with alcohol and drug abuse, disappearance, and suicide as do urban youth. Severe weather and natural catastrophes can touch everyone.

Investing time in personal security and safety is as important in rural settings as in urban ones. Consider investing in alarm system to monitor for smoke, fire, intrusion and other hazards.

- Be certain that all the outside doors on your home and outbuildings are made of solid wood or metal.

- Planning for severe weather or incremental security often feature complementary safety benefits. Build or enhance an interior room or cellar location as a safe room with fortified construction that can resist natural disasters or intruders. Equip the room with non-perishable food, water, and emergency supplies including a radio, flashlights, and medical kit. Consider a generator to provide minimal energy requirements for perishable food refrigeration, a safety rated space heater, lights, and communications recharging.
- Install and use dead bolt locks on all the outside doors on your home and outbuildings.
- Secure any sliding doors with commercial locks, with a metal or wood dowel in the door track (to jam the door in case someone tries to pry it open), and with screws in the top frame (to prevent anyone from lifting the door out of its frame).
- Install and use the locks on your windows, including the basement windows.
- Keep the area well-lighted at night. Install motion detection, photo cell, or timer lights to detect and deter trespassers and properly light doors and pathways for household members and guests.
- Consider integrating closed circuit television with glass break or motion detection sensors with an alarm monitoring agency. A siren may be used to drive off intruders and alert neighbors.
- Keep trees and shrubs well pruned to reduce hiding places for burglars.
- Keep fences in good repair. Secure access roads with gates or cables stretched between posts that have been cemented into the ground.
- Post **No Hunting**, **No Trespassing, Security Surveillance Monitoring**, and **Beware of Dog** signs to let intruders know that you are on the alert and prepared to hold them accountable.
- Explore insurance discounts for fire and security protection.
- Mark your tools, equipment, and livestock. Some new farm and construction machinery features GPS locators. Investigate aftermarket GPS capabilities to locate your equipment or prize bull if it is stolen. Work with your local public safety agency or newspaper to communicate community-wide crime or risk mitigation best practices.
- Secure gas pumps, gas tanks, storage bins, and grain elevators with sturdy padlocks or dead bolts. Monitor or alarm high value inventory with smart security devices including analytic closed circuit television (cctv) and intrusion detection devices.

- Keep guns, ammunition and non-lethal weapons in securely available, fire-rated lock boxes.
- Do not leave tools in the back of a truck. Lock them inside and out of sight.
- Do not leave keys in your vehicles.
- Educate children early about the all-hazard risk mitigation from crime prevention to operating farm machinery.
- If you must leave equipment in a field overnight, rather than locking it in a barn or shed, you can still minimize the likelihood of theft. Place machines and equipment in locations where you or your neighbor can see them. Disable the machine, if possible, by removing the battery, distributor, or rotor.
- Store harvested crops in protected and locked locations.
- Consider marking grain or other crops with non-toxic confetti that can be removed by storage or processing facilities.
- Keep a record of your valuable timber. Mark each piece with a paint stripe.
- Keep storage areas neat and well-organized so that any theft will be noticed immediately.
- Help your community schools start programs in crime prevention and responses to alcohol and drug abuse.
- Work with your neighbors to watch each other's property when you are away on business or vacation. Pick up each other's mail, check the property on a daily basis, park an extra vehicle in plain sight and communicate the impression that the premises are inhabited and everyday routines are being followed.
- Start a Neighborhood Watch group. Use radios or cellular telephones to patrol areas and report suspicious activities.
- Ask equipment dealers and farm suppliers to display crime prevention information.
- If you hire employees, check their references carefully.

2.7 WHEN YOU ARE DRIVING

This section has tips for helping you be more secure in your car. For more information, see Chapter 7: When You Travel and Chapter 8: Automobiles.

- Maintain your car in good operating condition to reduce the chance of a breakdown.

- Consider subscribing to an emergency road side assistance service.
- Keep an aerosol tire inflator, working jack, spare tire, road flares, non-perishable food and water and blankets in your car in case of an emergency.
- Consider installing a car alarm, remote door locks and hand free mobile communication capability.
- Keep your gas tank at least one-quarter full to reduce the chance that you will run out of gas.
- Store change for making phone calls in the glove compartment.
- Have your keys and alarm fob in your hand when you approach your car.
- As you approach your car, glance around it and under it. When you reach your car, check both the front and back seats before you get in.
- Glance at the vehicles parked next to your car. Be wary of any vans parked next to you. Vans are often used in abductions. If you have a flat tire and someone is sitting in a vehicle you should be on high alert.
- Keep valuables out of sight. Store your valuables in the trunk before you leave.
- Lock the doors and keep the windows rolled up at all times, whether you are in the car or not.
- Never leave your keys in your car.
- Never pick up a hitchhiker of either gender.
- Unless it is a life-threatening emergency, do not stop for a motor-ist in trouble. Note an intersection or highway mile marker or exit proximity. Pull over at a safe opportunity or contact public safety via handsfree mobile communications to report a motorist in need.
- If your car breaks down, raise the hood and attach a white piece of cloth (like a handkerchief) to the antenna or hood. Stay inside the car. Advise public safety or your subscription roadside assistance.
- If someone stops to help you during a breakdown, do not get out of the car and do not let the stranger in. Never accept a ride. Ask the other motorist to call for assistance if you do not have a mobile phone.
- After a minor accident, especially one where there was little reason for the accident or there are two or more people in the other car, stay alert. If you feel uncomfortable, do not get out of your car. Motion for the other car to follow you to a police station or a

well-lit emergency stop area. Call for public safety assistance before getting out of the vehicle

- If someone uses force to get into your car, do not allow yourself to be taken somewhere else. Get out of the car and run.
- If someone intentially flattens your tires, get in the car lock it and call the police. A vehicle with four flat tires can outrun a man on foot.
- When you drop off friends, relatives, or babysitters make certain that they are safely inside their home before you drive away.
- When possible, travel with someone else. People traveling alone are more likely to be targets of carjacking.
- If you become involved in a carjacking attempt, relinquish your vehicle without hesitation and call the police immediately.
- Use grocery assistance and valet parking and parking garage escort services after dark.
- Carefully choose well lit and busy businesses that feature security patrols and systems for necessary late night purchases or cash transactions.

2.8 COMPLETING ERRANDS

When you are out completing errands, stay alert to your surroundings.

- Choose clothing and footwear that allow you to move freely.
- Do not overburden yourself with packages so that your view is obstructed or you find it difficult to react.
- If possible, go out with someone else. There is safety in numbers.
- Be certain someone knows where you are going and when you expect to return.
- Carry sufficient change for emergency telephone calls and for using public transportation.
- Do not carry more cash than you can afford to lose.
- Do not wear expensive jewelry.
- Carry your wallet in your front pocket or in an inside jacket pocket. If you carry a purse, carry it in front of you and hold it close.
- Walk briskly and with confidence. Use well-traveled and well-lighted streets. Stay away from doorways, alleys, and obstructions. Avoid dark or wooded areas.
- If you use public transportation, sit near the driver if possible.
- When you go out for entertainment, remember to stay alert to your surroundings. See the section *Going Out For Entertainment* in this chapter for more information.

2.8.1 Using an Automated Teller Machine (ATM)

Automated teller machines (ATMs) can be areas of relatively high risk because of the availability of cash and because the user's back is not protected.

- Avoid using ATMs that are streetside, poorly lit or feature minimum surveillance by security, passers-by or public safety patrols. Use busy ATMs that are well lit, under security surveillance and are patrolled. Busy well lit indoor locations are best in banks or shopping malls that feature additional security.
- Avoid using ATMs at night, if possible. Most attacks occur between 8 p.m. and 2 a.m.
- Have someone accompany you whenever possible. Look for loiterers before committing to a transaction.
- Fill out any forms before you use the ATM. Have your card ready when you approach the ATM.
- Stand directly in front of the machine so that no one can see your personal identification number when you key it in.
- Avoid displaying cash in public. Count your cash when you return to your car, your home, or another safe place.
- If anything suspicious happens while you are making a transaction, cancel the transaction immediately, retrieve your card, and leave.
- If you notice anyone following you after you leave an ATM, go to the nearest public area. Use your mobile phone to alert trusted others of your location and situation.

2.9 GOING OUT FOR ENTERTAINMENT

Going out to a movie, dinner, a sporting event, or a social event at night makes you particularly vulnerable as a target for crime. Carrying money, wearing dressy clothes, and the fact that you are relaxed and out to have a good time are all factors that could increase your risk.

Here are some things to remember:

- When possible, go out with someone else. You are less likely to be a target when you are in a group.
- Take a cab, use a car service or have a designated driver if you are drinking.
- Be certain someone knows where you are going and when you expect to return.

- Do not carry large amounts of cash. Use a credit card.
- Carry sufficient change for emergency telephone use and for using public transportation.
- At sporting events, be wary of pushing, shoving, and fighting. Pickpockets often begin their theft by running into their victims.
- Be wary of intoxicated people and drivers.
- Practically any event may be the target for a demonstration. Be alert to groups that may be agitating for media coverage.
- Be particularly careful if you wear expensive jewelry. Use valet parking if available, and only give the attendant your car keys, not the entire key chain.
- Do not leave valuables in your car.
- Do not attach your home address to your key chain. Use your work or email address to prevent a stranger in possession of your keys from knowing where you live.
- Avoid parking garages unless they are busy, well lit, and surveilled or patrolled by security.
- Carry your wallet in your front pocket or in an inside jacket pocket. If you carry a purse, carry it in front of you and hold it close.
- Walk purposefuly and with confidence. Use well-traveled and well-lighted streets. Stay away from doorways, alleys, and obstructions. Avoid dark or wooded areas.
- Do not let alcohol impair your judgment. Stay under control.
- Do not carry on conversations with panhandlers.
- Be aware of your personal space in a nightclub.

2.10 WHEN YOU TRAVEL OUT OF TOWN

When you travel out of town, for either business or pleasure, always let someone else know your itinerary: where you are going, when you expect to arrive, when you expect to return, where you will be staying, and a contact telephone number in the event of an emergency. Message that you are safely on the way, aboard your bus, flight or train for departure or have arrived at your destination.

For more information about travel security, see *Hotel Security* in this chapter, Chapter 7: When You Travel, and Chapter 8: Automobiles.

- Plan ahead. If you are traveling by car, get a map and plan your route. Use a GPS and handsfree mobile communications. Check the car to be certain that it is running well and that all the tires are sound.

- Consider a new model rental car with trip emergency assistance or GPS navigation.
- Travel with a companion, if possible.
- Stop your mail and paper delivery or have a trusted neighbor pick them up on a daily basis. Have a friend keep an eye on your home while you are gone. Invite a neighbor to park a car in your driveway.
- If you are traveling internationally. Check the travel risks of your destination with a reputable travel assistance firm. Determine if precautionary vaccines or medical precautions are required. Inquire about low cost medical, security and trip interruption insurances.
- Get credit cards and mobile telephone service pre-approved but do not take more credit cards than you will need. Consider a low-cost telephone rental overseas to avoid unnecessary cost and message your trip progress will itinerary followers.
- Carry a copy of your passport, driver's license, credit cards, separate from other valuables. Leave a copy with a trusted friend or associate in case you need to replace them.
- Plan on leaving your passport, credit card and some cash in a hotel room safe or safety deposit box at your destination. If police or other officials ask for your papers, offer your copy of your passport that is locked up for safekeeping back at the hotel.
- Stay in a recommended hotel if you are unfamiliar with the city. Read well informed travel literature and blogs regarding local health, man-made and natural travel hazards.
- Pick up a card with the hotel manager's name, address and telephone number in case of emergency. Use hotel recommended car services or public transportation.
- Request a room off the main street and three to five floors up (for extra security or fire rescue) if there is elevator service. Inspect the place you are planning to stay carefully before you unpack. Count the number of doors to fire escapes and ensure they are unobstructed. Be certain that all the locks work.
- A stout rubber doorstop is a travel security essential. Placed under the inside of your door it provides formidable added security.
- Do not overburden yourself with luggage so that your view is obstructed or you cannot move freely. Backpacks are ideal. Pack extra food and water if you are hiking or in a seismic area.

- Do not carry a large amount of cash. Avoid unnecessary laptops, gadgets and accessories that will make you an attractive target for a street robbery or cafe theft.
- Be certain that your luggage is locked or checked. Defer maid service if you do not want someone in your room. Use hotel provided safety deposit boxes or room safes for valuables. Use luggage straps. Do not leave your luggage unattended.
- Do not look distracted or lost when you are in an airport, at a busy public place or tourist attraction, or on a crowded street. Be alert for pickpockets and thieves.
- Watch out for accidents that might have been staged, and be wary of strangers needing assistance or offering to do you a favor. (For example, a spilled drink, someone offering to take your picture, someone asking for directions or the correct time, or a pedestrian jumping in front of your car.) A criminal hoping to rob or assault you must get close enough to do so, and will probably try to distract you first.

2.11 HOTEL SECURITY

Hotels can have less than ideal security for a variety of reasons. Search the web for consumer ratings. Choose your hotel carefully, paying particular attention to its location. Consult your travel service for a recommendation within your budget. Check out the premises when you arrive. Valet park. If you feel that the hotel is not secure, move to a different hotel as soon as you can.

- The most important aspect of hotel security is the local environment and location of the hotel.
- When you check in, be certain that no one sees your room number or overhears an announcement by the room clerk. If someone does, get a different room.
- Do not stay in a hotel where the doors to the rooms lead directly outside. A room with direct access to the outside makes it easier for someone to track your movements and/or break-in. Upper floor rooms, between floors three and five, insulate the traveler from street-level crime yet still facilitate fire or emergency medical evacuation.
- Avoid rooms on floors higher than the fifth floor, since most fire truck ladders do not reach beyond that point.

- Do not display your guest room keys or leave them unattended in a public place such as a dining room, the pool, or a workout room.
- Stay at a hotel that uses coded electronic cards instead of keys, if possible. These cards are more secure than keys. Carry a stout rubber doorstop and supplement room security by placing it securely beneath your door.
- Before you tip the bellman or unpack, check your room for security integrity, damages or other conditions that you find unsuitable. Check all the locks in your room (door and window locks) to ensure that they all work. Look for lock set or door frame damage that may indicate the door has been forced. Do not stay in a room that has locks that do not work.
- Once you have checked the room, ask the bellman or check your room location map (usually on the back of the door) for fire exit locations. Count the doors to the fire exit in case you have to navigate an unlit hallway in an emergency. Place the **Do Not Disturb** sign on the outside and lock the door with both the dead bolt or chain.
- You may want to consider bringing your own locking devices and alarms such as a door block or a sound alarm with a magnetic contact switch.
- As you return to your room, if you believe that someone is following you, do not go directly to your room. Walk past your room to see what the other person will do.
- When leaving your room, hang the **Do Not Disturb** sign on the door and leave the light and the radio or TV on. Thieves look for rooms that look and sound unoccupied.
- Request an escort to your room or the parking area if you feel uncomfortable.
- If hotel maintenance, room service, or security appears unexpectedly at your door, do not let them in. Verify with the front desk that they have a reason to enter your room.

2.11.1 Elevator Security
- Check the elevator before entering. If you feel uneasy about anyone in the elevator, wait for the next one.
- When you are waiting for the elevator to arrive, stand away from the door to avoid being pushed inside when the elevator arrives.

- When you enter the elevator, stand near the control panel. This will enable you to press the alarm button and as many of the other floor buttons as possible in case you have a problem.
- Wait until the other passengers press their floor buttons before you press the button for your floor.
- Stay alert. Look around at the other passengers. If anyone makes you uncomfortable, get off at the next floor. Do not continue to your room. Go to the lobby and request an escort.
- If you are accosted, push all the buttons on the control panel, including the **Alarm** button. Do not push the **Stop** button. Yell **Fire** or **Help** and try to get off at each floor.
- Often it is best not to ride with just one other person in an elevator if that person is a stranger and your instincts or intuition make you wary. An elevator that has a moderate number of people is the safest.
- Report any elevator malfunction to the hotel staff immediately.

2.12 DURING THE HOLIDAYS

Burglars, muggers, and pickpockets are more active during the holiday season because there are many opportunities presented by people as they rush around, buy gifts, become tired or distracted, and, in general, exercise less caution than usual.

Additional holiday-related security information can be found in other topics in this chapter; in particular, *Completing Errands* and *Going Out for Entertainment*.

- When you shop, stay alert to what is happening around you. Go with a companion, if possible. If you shop at night, park in well-lighted areas that are surveilled and patrolled by security or public safety personnel.
- Always lock your car. Lock your valuables in the trunk.
- Do not carry large amounts of cash or credit cards you are not using. Keep a record of your transactions.
- Do not over-burden yourself with packages. Keep your arms as free as possible.
- Teach your children how to go to a store clerk or store security if they become separated from you while shopping.

- Before you leave make certain your home is secure. Take a few minutes to ensure that all doors and windows are locked before going out.
- If you are going away for a few days, use automatic timers to turn radios and lights on and off intermittently. Have a friend collect your mail and papers while you are gone or have delivery stopped. Arrange for snow removal or lawn maintenance.
- Illuminated and unattended Christmas trees may pose an inordinate fire hazard.
- Do not display gifts where they can be easily seen from a door or window.
- If you have house guests, be certain that they know and follow your security rules.
- Update your home's inventory of electronic equipment (stereos, TVs, VCRs, etc.), sporting goods, computers, and other valuables. Take photos, or use a videotape to record the inventory.
- Mark your valuables. If your home is burglarized, your insurance claim will be easier to process and you will have a better chance of recovering your losses.
- "Follow me" software and applications are available for personal computers, smartphones and other electronic gadgets.

2.13 AT WORK

This section contains a few tips for personal protection at work. For more detailed information, see Chapter 6: Workplace Safety and Security.

- Protect both the people and the assets of the organization by wearing proper ID and by being aware of people who are not authorized to be in restricted areas. Ask persons not badged or improperly badged if you may help them. Escort them to reception or security for a proper credential. Report those who resist site protocol as a suspicious person. Be prepared to provide a detailed description.
- Take responsibility for ensuring that electronic and security systems work as designed. Do not prop open secure doors and do not let unauthorized people enter an area. Escort unauthorized persons out of an area if necessary. Keep passwords and key combinations confidential. Report any unusual situation to site security or need-to-know management.

- If you work before or after normal business hours, turn the radio on low and leave other workstation lights on so that it appears that you are not alone. Keep the doors to the exterior locked.
- When you leave work request a security escort service if one is provided or accompany a co-worker to parking. Make certain your mobile phone is programmed to call site security or the local public safety agency in the event of an emergency.
- Park your car in a well-lighted area.

2.14 STREET SOLICITORS AND PANHANDLERS

Every day, thousands of people panhandle and solicit for donations in the streets of major cities around the world. Most of us provide spare change without really thinking about it. Experts say that the spare change does not help; in some cases it actually hurts both the panhandler and the community.

- Spare change may actually enable panhandlers to avoid dealing with the situations that have put them on the street (drugs, unemployment, mental health, etc.).
- Panhandling can be "big business." Skilled panhandlers have been known to take in significant amounts of money each day.
- Panhandling can undermine the sense of safety and friendliness of a community. Successful panhandling encourages others to move into the area or take up the practice. Communities can see their quality of life decline due to large-scale panhandling.
- Panhandlers rarely become aggressive. Do not be afraid to say **No** to a request.
- If you see a panhandler in a work area, report the incident immediately to management.
- Most panhandlers need help. The best way to help them out of their situation is to donate, volunteer, and advocate for the local and national institutions that provide shelter and food for the homeless, assistance for the unemployed, and counseling for mental and emotional problems.
- Instead of giving spare change, make a commitment of money or time to an organization that is working on the problems faced by people who need to panhandle, and then refer panhandlers to those agencies. Tell them where they can get help.

Assault and Sexual Assault

3.1 OVERVIEW

Protecting yourself and others from assault and sexual assault involves three main components: prevention, deterrence, and physical resistance. Prevention covers all the things you can do to avoid dangerous situations. Deterrence involves your actions when you are confronted by someone who may assault you. Physical resistance addresses actions you take to defend yourself.

In this chapter, prevention, and deterrence are combined under the *Reducing Your Risk* section. Physical resistance is covered under *Self-Defense*.

The first topic in this chapter is *Develop a Personal Strategy*. There is no single way to adapt the methods of prevention, deterrence, and physical resistance to an individual's personal situation that is always right. It is important that you make a personal choice about the way in which you will handle a difficult encounter.

Many of the topics in this chapter deal with sexual assault, how to reduce your risk, and what to do in case you are sexually assaulted. The last section addresses assault situations that are associated with a mugging or robbery. Most of the precautions apply to all assault situations, whether sexual or otherwise.

3.2 DEVELOP A PERSONAL STRATEGY

Imagine yourself arriving home from work about an hour later than usual because of last-minute details on tomorrow's presentation. As you pull into your garage, you are listening to one of your favorite oldies on the radio while daydreaming about next month's vacation plans. You turn off the engine, grab your briefcase, and open the car door to get out. Suddenly, you are knocked down and pushed back into your car. Your heart is pounding and a chill comes over you as you realize that *you are being attacked.*

How would you respond? What is your mind set going to be? How will you try to defuse the attacker? Will you physically resist or try to escape? And how could this situation have been avoided?

Visualizing yourself in an assault is frightening, but it is one way of understanding your own reaction. Developing a personal strategy is really a commitment to reducing your risk and preparing yourself for handling a situation in which you have been attacked.

A personal strategy begins with learning how to avoid dangerous situations and knowing quick and effective techniques for deterring the assailant and for defending yourself. As you read the following sections, place yourself in specific real-life situations. Then make mental or written notes of the things you can do to prevent assault and the self-defense strategies that are the best for you, keeping in mind your own capabilities. Begin practicing what you have learned at home, at work, and while traveling.

By thinking through the issues and designing an overall plan, you will develop that "sixth sense" about dangerous situations and build personal confidence. You will also start to make realistic assessments of whether to run or fight, whether you want to use a weapon, and the best ways to divert or diffuse an attack.

3.3 REDUCING YOUR RISK

Reducing your risk of an assault or a sexual assault involves both an awareness of your surroundings and the personal confidence that you are not going to be a victim. Many jurisdictions require convicted sexual predators to register with local public safety or law enforcement agencies. Public records are often available to inform you of predators living in your postal zipcode, neighborhood or building.

Even if you take every preventative step, you will not be able to completely eliminate all risk of assault. You can, however, greatly diminish the chance that you will be a victim of an assault. If you are assaulted, you still have many options (see the next section, *Self-Defense*).

This section covers four risk reduction areas that are under your direct control:

- Stay alert to your surroundings. Avoid situations that are likely to be dangerous. Pay attention to your intuition.
- Be aware of your feelings about situations as they develop. Trust your instincts.
- Maintain your personal space. You can take direct action to make it difficult for someone to attack you.
- Be assertive. Use body language and verbal aggressiveness to stay in control of a situation.

3.3.1 Stay Alert to Your Surroundings

The best thing you can do to promote your own personal security is to stay alert and be aware of your surroundings, your neighborhood, and your community.

- Pay attention to what is going on around you. Be careful not to be distracted. Many assaults start out with an ambiguous social situation where the attacker uses an innocent question or request to distract you while moving into your personal space.
- Do not put yourself in situations that have the potential for danger, and if you sense that a situation is becoming dangerous, get out of it immediately.
- You may need to change your living environment completely by moving to a new city or a new location. You may need to change your attitude toward the people around you and how they treat each other.
- Use your common sense. Street sense and common sense are just about the same thing.
- Be confident of your own capabilities, but do not put yourself in situations that you cannot handle.
- Use this guideline for suggestions and advice on how to structure situations to reduce your risk.

3.3.2 Trust Your Instincts

Most people have a good sixth sense that tells them when something is not right. If someone gets on an elevator that makes you afraid, get off the elevator. Report any suspicious persons, vehicles, and conditions that make you afraid.

- Do not be polite when a stranger encroaches on your personal space and you want the person to leave. Tell the person directly and without any hesitation to move away from you.
- It is important that you trust your instincts about what is dangerous. Many people who have been assaulted report that they felt that something was wrong, but they did not do anything about it until it was too late.

3.3.3 Maintain Your Personal Space

For most people and cultures, a distance of about one arm's length is a comfortable personal space. For personal protection, however, the distance needs to be about twice as large. Since an attacker can lunge at you to get you into his grasp, keeping about six feet between yourself and a person who is making you uncomfortable provides you with a safety zone.

The simple fact is that, unless an attacker is using a gun, he must be able to reach you to harm you.

- If a stranger gets too close to you, move away. Put an object such as a table, a bench, a car, or another person between yourself and the person who is making you uncomfortable.
- Since most attackers use an ambiguous social situation to get close to a potential victim, do not be afraid to make the first move in interpreting an ambiguous, uncomfortable situation as one that is potentially dangerous.

3.3.4 Be Assertive

Use your voice and your body language to maintain an assertive posture.

- Make brief eye contact with a stranger who is approaching you. Let the person know that you are aware of him and his actions are being noticed.

- If someone starts to talk to you and you do not want to have a conversation, tell him clearly and without hesitation to move away from you and that you do not want to talk to him.

3.4 SELF-DEFENSE

Self-defense can take many forms. Depending on the situation, striking back physically, resisting verbally, fleeing, or submitting can all be appropriate self-defense tactics.

Self-defense is a personal issue that requires you to make some decisions. You may decide to use only verbal resistance and look for a chance to escape, or you may decide to use physical resistance, which might include the use of a weapon.

If you decide to carry a lethal or non-lethal weapon, seek proficiency if not expertise, with licensed, insured and competent trainers. Equip yourself with rated lockboxes for household or vehicle storage. Cypher lock boxes and equivalent devices enable responsible weapon owners near instant access while keeping them out of the hands of children and the casual thief.

Pepper gas and other non-lethal weapons may sufficiently impair an attacker from injuring you more seriously, successfully chasing you down or driving you off. Any weapon introduces a potential element of escalation and serious injury.

Use the self-defense strategy that works best for you. Not all strategies will work in every situation, but there are some common elements that may help you defend yourself.

- Keep a level head. Do not panic.
- Use verbal resistance and body language to tell a potential attacker that you are not an easy victim. Scream for help at the first possible chance.
- Stay calm and focus on your breathing. Most people tend to hold their breath when they are startled or tense. It is very difficult to take decisive action, like running or striking, if you are holding your breath. A good way to start your breathing when you are frightened is to shout **No!** or **Stop!**

- **Do not resist if someone wants only money or valuables. Give them up!** Obey a robber's reasonable commands.
- Never let an attacker remove you from the place where he first approached you. Your chances of being hurt seriously are much greater if you allow yourself to be taken to a remote place.
- Pretend to cooperate if you need to stall for time. You may be able to talk your way out of a situation or gain an advantage with surprise.
- Use all your senses. Observe the attacker's appearance. Look for differentiating features carefully, one at a time (hair color, eye color, clothing, height, weight, scars), and make mental notes. Shoes, clothing and headgear often feature distinctive logos, stains or wear and tear. Listen for voice peculiarities including tones, accents and speech impediments. Alcohol or marijuana smell may provide valuable information of your assailant's alertness for a surprise counterattack or escape.
- Program your mobile to call 911 or invest in a smartphone app that will call police and provide your GPS coordinates even if you are in flight.
- Do everything you can to disrupt the attacker's plan. A potential assailant can often get confused and discouraged if things do not work out as planned.

3.4.1 Using Sound

Crime prevention professionals believe that sound is one of the best self-defense tools. Some studies have shown that many people who scream have escaped from an attacker. Loud sound – yelling, talking, or using a sound device – tells the attacker of your unwillingness to be a victim, startles him, and draws attention to the crime scene.

- Your voice is the sound device you always have with you. Shout at the assailant in a direct tone, using short, sharp words like: **Stop that right now!** or **Get away from me!** or **Do not touch me!**
- Scream. Generally, the louder and longer the scream, the better it works as a deterrent.
- Carry a whistle. A long, loud blast from a whistle can deter an attacker and summon help.
- Yell **Fire!** or **Help!** The word "Fire" will attract a quicker response from strangers.

- Consider a shriek alarm or personal siren. Carry one with you and keep one next to your bed at night.

3.4.2 Striking an Assailant
The choice of whether to use physical self-defense is a personal one. If you contemplate fighting your way out of an assault, train with competent instructors and consider martial arts or kickboxing for personal fitness. There is no way of predicting the actions of your attacker if you fight back. *You must decide whether you will resist an attacker who has a weapon, since your response must depend on your assessment of the situation.*

- Do not strike immediately. Chances are your attacker has the first advantage. Wait until you can strike him when he is off guard. Surprise is essential.
- During the initial confrontation, the attacker is hyped-up by adrenaline and will respond more aggressively to resistance on your part.
- If possible, use items in your purse or close at hand − a fingernail file, hairspray, keys, or other object − or try to scratch your assailant in the face or eyes.
- Punch your attacker in the throat, or kick him in the knees or groin. Be careful not to lose your balance when you strike.

3.5 RAPE
Rape is an act of violence. It is an attempt to control and degrade a person by using sex as a weapon.

- Rape can happen to anyone − children, students, wives, mothers, working women, grandmothers, the rich, the poor, boys, and men.
- A rapist can be anyone − a classmate, a coworker, a neighbor, a delivery or service person, someone who is attractive or ugly, or outgoing or shy. Often a rapist is a friend or family member.
- Rapists continue to commit rape until they are caught.

3.5.1 Using Awareness to Avoid Rape
Stay alert to and aware of your surroundings in order to avoid situations that are potentially dangerous.

- Stay alert. Be aware of your surroundings. Do not let alcohol or drugs cloud your judgment. If a situation makes you feel uncomfortable, get out of it immediately.
- Keep your doors and windows locked. Many of the world's most infamous predators have gained access to their victims through open or unlocked doors and windows. Do not open your doors to strangers. If you come home and a window or door is open or broken, do not go in the house. Call the police.
- Be wary of such isolated spots as parks, garages, hiking trails, laundry rooms, parking lots, and offices after business hours. Do not walk or jog by yourself, especially at night. If you must walk or jog at night seek a trusted companion and carry your cell phone and a sturdy flashlight.
- If your car breaks down, stay in it if it is safe to do so and call or message public safety or emergency assistance. Ask good samaritans to call for you. Do not stop for another motorist with car trouble. Note an exit, landmark or milemarker and advise public safety as soon as it is safe to do so. Do not hitchhike and do not pick up hitchhikers.
- If you think you are being followed, either on foot or when you are driving, make extra turns or change directions. If you are still being followed, go to the nearest busy, public, well-lit place, such as a restaurant, theater, or open store. Use your hands-free communications to alert others.

3.5.2 Handling a Rape Attempt

How you handle a rape attempt depends on the situation, your physical and emotional state, and the rapist's personality. There is no single right or wrong way to handle the situation. You may resist or submit. Take whatever course of action is necessary to assure your survival.

- Studies have shown that women who fight back often are injured, but are somewhat less likely to be raped. Other studies suggest that it is easier to recover from an injury than from a sexual assault. However, sometimes fighting aggravates the rapist and leads to severe injury or death.
- Stay calm. Look for identifying characteristics. Often the potential rapist is someone with whom you are familiar or know well.
- Stall for time so that you can assess your options.

- You may be able to talk your way out of the situation by telling him that you have a disease, or by getting him to feel guilt or remorse.
- Noise can be an effective deterrent. If you choose to carry a personal alarm or other sound device, use it. Yell **Fire!** or **Help!** as loud as you can.
- Look for a way to escape. Disrupt the rapist's plan and try to run away.
- If the attacker is alone and does not have a weapon, you may be able to fight your way out of the situation. Strike at his throat, eyes, or groin. Use any available weapon you can find, including your keys, a pen or pencil, or other objects in your purse or within reach.
- It is important that you decide on a defense strategy that works for you. There is no one right or wrong way to handle a rape attempt.

3.5.3 Surviving Rape

If you are raped, do not accept the blame for what happened. You are the victim. The rapist is the criminal and is solely responsible.

- Do not shower, bathe, douche, or change your clothes immediately after the incident. Do not discard any physical evidence.
- Report any rape or sexual assault attempt immediately to the police, hospital, or to a rape crisis center. The sooner you report the assault, the greater the chances are that the rapist will be caught. Since rapists continue to commit sexual assaults until they are caught, you will be helping to reduce the chances that someone else will be victimized.
- Go immediately to the hospital emergency room or to your doctor for medical care. Go with a friend if possible.
- Ask a friend, a family member, a school counselor, or a counselor from a rape center to go with you to the police.
- Seek professional help and counseling to help you work through the feelings of anger, helplessness, shame, and fear that are caused by rape. It helps to talk to someone, whether the rape happened recently or years ago.

3.5.4 Take a Stand Against Rape

Rape is a crime that destroys the fabric of the community. Take a stand against rape by:

- Believing the victim. If someone tells you that he or she has been raped, believe it. Help to report the crime and to get counseling.

- Challenging society's acceptance of rape as a lesser crime. Educate your friends and family. Volunteer at a rape crisis center.
- Working with your Neighborhood Watch group, church, school, employer, or civic organization to sponsor a workshop on preventing rape. Be certain that the workshop is for both women and men.
- Keeping an eye on the media and entertainment. Do not allow movies and television to show violence against women. Call or write to the station, the sponsors, or the studio to protest any depiction of the myth that women enjoy rape.
- Providing positive feedback and public commendation to any news or media organization when it accurately reports the realities of rape.
- Joining organizations that are working to reduce the portrayal of violence on television and in movies. Rape is a crime of violence.

3.6 DATE RAPE

Rapists are not always strangers. When a date, a friend, or a fiancé forces someone to have sex, it is not romance or passion. It is a serious crime of violence that is also a betrayal of trust.

Date rape happens because people still believe in sexual stereotypes that teach men to be aggressive and women to be passive, that say it is okay for a man to demand sex in return for buying a woman dinner or gifts, that women really mean **Yes** when they say **No**, or that once a woman has had sex with a man she cannot expect him to take **No** for an answer.

3.6.1 Preventing Date Rape

As a woman, you can help prevent date rape by:

- Taking a close look at the men around you. Be wary of men who attempt to belittle you, control your choice of friends and activities, and have feelings of hostility toward women.
- Not letting alcohol or drugs cloud your ability to make sensible judgments about people and situations.
- Being careful on first dates and blind dates. Check out the man through friends or acquaintances. Carry sufficient money for phone calls and transportation. Meet at a public place, such as a movie theater, a restaurant, or a coffee house. Double dates offer a safe way to meet and date someone for the first time.

- Talking openly about sex as a relationship progresses. Set up the expectation that you are in control of your own body and that you will make decisions about your sexual involvement.
- Getting out of any situation that makes you uneasy for any reason.
- Trusting your feelings. Pay attention to your sixth sense about people and their intentions.

As a man, you can help prevent date rape by:

- Exploring your attitudes and the attitudes of your friends toward women.
- Accepting a woman's decision when she says **No**. Do not view **No** as a challenge.
- Not letting alcohol or drugs cloud your judgment about what is appropriate behavior.
- Understanding that rape is a serious crime of violence with serious consequences.
- Not allowing yourself to be drawn into a gang rape at parties, after sporting events, in fraternities, or in bars.
- Summoning the courage to defend a victim or at least reporting an assault in progress
- Seeking counseling if you have difficulty controlling feelings of violence and aggression.

3.6.2 If Date Rape Happens to You or to Someone You Know

If date rape happens to you or to someone you know, see the guidelines included in the "Surviving Rape" subsection under *Rape* earlier in this chapter. It's important to remember not to blame the victim. The blame belongs solely to the criminal who committed the act.

3.7 HIGH SCHOOLS AND COLLEGE CAMPUSES

Understand the risk history of the school, and surrounding neighborhoods as well as its public safety resources. Participate in emergency drills for fire, severe weather and active shooter. Make certain you have emergency communication options. Know the basics for emergency reporting, shelter in place and evacuation.

Unfortunately, high schools and colleges are experiencing increased occurrences of assault and sexual assault. Common sense will help reduce the chances that you will be the victim of an assault. If someone is talking about injuring others and has the means to do so report them to the public safety or campus security unit.

- Stay alert to your surroundings.
- Avoid dark or isolated places.
- Use escort services after dark.
- If you think you are being followed, change directions and go to a well-lit public place where there are people.
- Program your phone for mobile emergency notifications on and off campus.
- Do not walk, bike, or jog alone, especially after dark. There is safety in numbers. Move against traffic as a pedestrian and wear reflective materials or bright colors.
- If you choose to carry a personal alarm, sound device, or other legal personal security device, be certain that it is reliable, you are trained, and know how to use it.
- Do not let alcohol or drugs interfere with your ability to make sensible judgments about people and situations.
- Do not become involved in a dangerous situation just because your friends or acquaintances are doing it.
- Lock the public doors to student residences at night and on weekends. Do not prop open the outside doors. Meet visitors at the entrance.
- Do not allow strangers to enter your room. If they do enter, demand that they leave. If they do not leave, create noise and commotion, and leave quickly.
- If you live in an apartment building, avoid isolated areas such as basements, stairways, and laundry rooms when you are alone.
- Be careful of situations that can lead to date rape (see the topic *Date Rape* in this chapter).
- Contact campus security immediately if you feel you are in danger or if you have been accosted.
- Get involved with groups and organizations that promote awareness of issues related to the problems of assault and sexual assault in high schools and on college campuses.

3.8 PROTECTING CHILDREN

Ascertain if there is a public record of known predators in your neighborhood. Protecting children from assault and sexual assault requires that you help reduce the risks they face and that you teach them how to make good judgments when handling difficult situations.

Some of the best methods for teaching children include modeling and rehearsal. Children learn by watching and doing. You must set a good example by doing the things you want them to do (for example, routinely locking doors, answering the phone correctly, checking in with their plans and phoning or messaging their wherabouts, as well as not allowing conflicts to become violent: "Use your words").

You can also use role-playing and rehearsal of situations to teach children how to handle difficult situations (for example, when and how to provide their name, address, and phone number; how to call 911; how to use a smartphone or public phone; and what to do in case they get lost).

3.8.1 Start With the Basics
Be certain that your children know:

- What to do if they get lost in a store or a mall or become separated from you in a crowded place;
- How to call 911, use a public phone, and provide their complete name, address, and phone number;
- How to scream: "He is not my daddy!" or "She is not my mommy!" if picked up by a stranger;
- That they should never accept a ride or gifts from a stranger;
- How to distinguish between appropriate touching and inappropriate touching;
- Why telling about a secret that feels bad can be a good thing; and
- That they should tell you about people and situations that make them feel uncomfortable. If this happens, be certain to listen carefully.

3.8.2 At School and Play
- Predators go to where the children are: amusement parks, bus stops, church, libraries, playgrounds, public pools, public restrooms, and schools. Make certain that institutions that care for your children screen their personnel and train them to detect and report child predators.
- Encourage your children to walk and play with others. Children alone provide inviting targets. Be certain that they are taking the

safest routes to and from school. Go with them on the routes and show them the dangerous spots and the places they can go for help.
- Encourage neighbors to let the kids report in on arrival or departure.
- Be wary of any adult who takes a special interest in your child and has the opportunity to spend time alone with them. Children are often abused by trusted adults including child care givers, family members, neighbors, clergy, and teachers or other school personnel and volunteers.
- Teach your children to avoid dangerous places, such as vacant buildings, alleys, and playgrounds with broken equipment. Teach them to move away from a stranger's vehicle that slows on the street.
- Teach your children to settle arguments by communicating without violence. Remind them that bullying, teasing and taunting can hurt their friend's feelings and make enemies.
- Work with your children to keep watch on your neighborhood. Help them to talk about the things they see that make them and you uncomfortable, like the man who passed two adults walking their dogs to ask the kids for directions.
- Explore the school's policy for informing parents when children are absent or tardy, as well as the policy on releasing children into the custody of an adult other than a parent.
- Make certain your children have the benefit of attending a school or child care facility that is certified for all-hazards preparedness and emergency first aid.

3.8.3 At Home
- Ensure your children and childcare providers know how to report a life-safety emergency, can render first aid, and know how and where to shelter in place or evacuate for severe weather or a fire.
- Teach your children to never reveal that they are alone when they answer the door or the telephone.
- Instruct your children not to give out information about who is home, who is out, or how long they will be gone.
- Teach your children to always ask who is at the door before opening it.
- Make sure your children know to not let anyone into their yard, leave the yard or play area, or go into someone else's home or vehicle without your permission.

3.8.4 Participate in Identification Programs

Having a complete record of your children's identification is extremely helpful if they are missing.

- Have pictures, fingerprints, and descriptions of your children on file with their schools.
- Photograph your children with childcare providers and companions when traveling or before a field trip.
- Teach children how to identify callers, license plates, and other information that can be used to track strangers. If they can read logos on shirts, shoes, and caps, add those elements to a game of "I Spy."
- Plan for safe, prearranged meeting places where your children will go in case they are lost or in danger.
- Train or practice your family emergency plans with neighbors and their children.

3.9 IF YOU HAVE BEEN ASSAULTED

If you have been assaulted:

- Report the incident immediately to the police. Provide as much information about the attacker as you can.
- Get medical help. Go to an emergency room.
- Seek help at a counseling center if you feel traumatized.
- Seek victims assistance through your local municipal, county, province, state or federal public safety resources

CHAPTER 4

Children

4.1 OVERVIEW

Children have a natural trust in other people, particularly adults. It is difficult for parents to teach children how to balance trust with caution, but children need to know how to protect themselves and how to handle threatening situations.

The key to security for children is effective communication. An open and honest atmosphere at home and school allows children to:

- discuss sensitive matters;
- talk freely about their feelings and experiences; and
- learn to trust their instincts and their own good judgment in difficult situations.

An open and honest atmosphere contributes to the overall security and safety of children and to their understanding of risk mitigation. Most children grow up without ever experiencing severe physical harm. However, too many children are frightened by crime and violence or become victims.

Although children of all ages are vulnerable, they can be taught how to identify risks, how to avoid or mitigate many hazardous situations, and what to do if something does happen to them.

4.2 ABDUCTION, KIDNAPPING, AND RUNAWAYS

According to the latest comprehensive national study (1999), 800,000 children are reported missing annually in the United States.[1] Missing children face great risks, regardless of the reason for their disappearance.

Children disappear for many different reasons. However, in most cases, missing children are either runaways or victims of abduction. Many of the abductions are carried out by estranged family members.

4.2.1 Runaways

The majority of missing children are runaways. Running away is the way they deal with certain kinds of problems:

- Difficulty communicating with parents. Good communication between parent and child is often the key to preventing abduction and kidnapping;
- Physical, emotional, and sexual abuse.
- Fear of disappointing their parents.
- Emotional or physical neglect. Some children, called throwaways, are indirectly pressured by a parent to leave home.

4.2.2 Victims of Kidnapping

Kidnapping is usually performed by one of two types of abductors:

1. Parents who kidnap their own child to hurt a former spouse or because they believe the parent in custody is not capable of caring for the child.
2. Other abductors, whose motives may range from rape and murder to profit-making schemes, such as ransom, forced prostitution, and child pornography. Occasionally, people kidnap because they are not able to have children of their own.

---

[1]"Key Facts," The National Center for Missing and Exploited Children, accessed September 13, 2013, http://www.missingkids.com/KeyFacts.

Ascertain if there is public information regarding convicted child predators in your neighborhood from your local public safety agency. Remember that many have never been charged.

4.2.3 Protecting Children
Protecting children depends on good communication and a rational and consistent set of rules to provide guidance.

- When you talk to children about security issues, be sure that you present information simply and directly. Be careful to avoid frightening them unnecessarily.
- Set rules that are appropriate to each child's age and level of maturity.
- Review rules often to help keep them fresh in each child's mind. Use role-playing so that they can practice what has been taught.
- Listen to a child who tells you that he or she does not want to be with a particular person. Try to find out why the child feels this way.
- Encourage children to tell you if an adult has bothered them. Reassure them that you will believe them, and that you will protect them from harm.
- Show your concern and love through what you say and do. No matter how old children are, they need to know that they are loved.

4.2.4 Tips for Parents
- Teach your children how to use the telephone or other communications properly in emergencies. Have them practice making emergency calls.
- Understanding that sounding false alarms and engaging in high risk behavior puts them and first responders or others at unnecessary peril is a lesson well learned. Well trained and savvy children can influence friends and adults to avoid risk. Asking if everyone is buckled before starting a vehicle (and ensuring that they are) will likely be adopted and repeated.
- Know your children's friends. Teach them to look out for each other.
- Be sure your children always know where you are and how to reach you.
- Develop an information file for your children that includes a recent photo, vital statistics, and medical information.

- When you are in public, always keep your children in sight. Plan with your children what to do if you are separated.
- Do not print a child's name in large letters on clothing or lunch boxes.
- Establish a code word that only your children and someone designated to pick up your children in an emergency knows. Establish the code word firmly by using a few role-playing situations.
- Check carefully the references of those responsible for your children. Don't hesitate to require a criminal background check.

4.2.5 Tips for Children

As a child, you can reduce your risk by following some guidelines:

- Know your address including zip code and your phone number including your area code. Extra marks for memorizing a telephone number of a grandparent or relative out of town.
- Let your parents know about anything or anyone that makes you afraid.
- Always tell your parents where you are going and when you expect to be back. Develop a check-in system that works for the children, you, responsible child care givers and your neighbors.
- There is safety in numbers. When you are playing, stay with friends that your parents know.
- If someone is hanging around a playground or schoolyard who makes you uneasy or gives you a bad feeling, tell your parents and your teacher.
- If someone grabs you, resist by kicking and screaming. Try to get away. Yell as loudly as can, "I do not know you!" or "You are not my mother!" or "You are not my father!" or "You are scaring me!" If someone is nearby, they will know that you are really in trouble.
- Anyone can be a kidnapper. Beware of strangers. Be very cautious of someone who makes great efforts to do you favors or become your friend.
- Never go near a vehicle with a stranger who is asking you to come closer.
- If you see a car following you, run to a neighbor's house or into a store. Never try to hide. Seek help from other people.
- Walk against traffic for safety.
- Ask your mom and dad what the family emergency plan is for accidents, a fire, or a natural disaster.

- Call your area Crime Stoppers program if you witness a crime and are afraid to tell anyone.[2] They will not ask for your name.

4.3 DAY CARE, SCHOOLS, AND PLAYGROUNDS

A large part of a child's life is spent at school, in the classroom, and on the playground. This section covers topics relating to the security and safety of school environments:

- Walking to and from school
- Using the bus
- In school
- Playgrounds, gyms, and locker rooms
- Parent involvement in school crime prevention and all-hazards risk preparedness

4.3.1 Walking to and from School

Be certain that children are taking the safest route to school. Walk the route with them, so that you can point out potential problems and show them places to seek safety in case of danger. Teach your children the basics for being safe and secure when they are walking:

- Stay alert. Watch out for situations that may be dangerous.
- Do not walk or play alone. Watch out for each other.
- Walk on the sidewalk near the curb and against the traffic.
- Let someone know if you are going to be home late.
- Carry a light and wear reflective clothing in the dark or for bad weather.
- Do not walk through vacant areas or places that are isolated.
- Never accept a ride from someone you and your parents do not know well.
- Know where the nearest house of a friend is, as well as where other safe places are.

4.3.2 Using the Bus

The basics for being secure while using the bus include the following:

[2]A list of Crime Stoppers programs by location can be found at http://www.crimestoppersusa.com/locate.htm.

- Know the time your bus comes to your stop. Be at the stop waiting for it. If you are late, you might miss the bus or get hurt as you run to catch it.
- Obey all traffic signs while walking to your bus stop.
- When you arrive at the bus stop, do not stand or play in the street or in other people's yards. Stay on the sidewalk by the bus stop.
- If it is dark outside, carry a flashlight and wear brightly colored clothing. Put your school books in a knapsack or backpack to make them easier to carry.
- Never let a stranger give you a ride. Wait for the bus and get on it. If you miss the bus, go back home.
- If you see a strange adult in a car near the bus stop without children tell the bus driver, your teacher, and your parents.

4.3.3 In School

The basics for being secure while in school include the following:

- Stay away from any stranger who may be hanging around by the restrooms, the playground, or any other area of the school.
- If someone makes you or a classmate afraid, tell your teacher and parents about it.
- If someone brings a gun, knife, or drugs to school tell a teacher or school security and your parents, even if you are not afraid.
- Do not leave school with anyone without your parent's permission.
- If somebody does something that makes you feel unsafe or uncomfortable, say "No!" Run away if the situation is dangerous, and tell a trusted adult what happened.
- Do not stay in any area, such as a restroom, a locker room, or a playground, if you are the only one there or if someone else makes you afraid.
- Always lock your locker.
- You can even make a class or club project out of making your school's lockers safer. Check with the school administration about buying good locks at a discount and then selling them to other students for a fund-raising project. You can raise money for a good cause, help protect your friends' valuables, and support the school's crime prevention activities all at the same time.

4.3.4 Parent Involvement in School All-Hazards Risk Mitigation

The benefits of parental involvement for ensuring all-hazards risk mitigation in our schools cannot be overstated. Some schools have organized programs already, and they always need volunteer help. Schools that do not have such a program would probably welcome the efforts of concerned parents to begin one.

The basic ways you can help make school more secure for your children include:

- Understanding the awareness level of the administration for the risk history of the campus for accidents, crime, seismic risk, severe weather or other hazards; and how they are prepared to mitigate those risks for children and staff. Do they have a plan? What are their resources? Would supplemental help from the PTA or other organizations make a difference for perceived risks?
- Your child's sense of safety and security depends on an environment like home, where risks and remedies are openly discussed.
- Determine if your children can carry a mobile phone or communicator to and from school.
- Assess the comparative risks of biking, bussing, walking or providing for other transportation.
- Get a secure lock for your child's locker if the school does not provide one. A good key lock is a better safeguard for property than a combination lock. The lock should have a rugged, laminated case and a 3/8″ shackle that resists being smashed. Look for a lock that does not release its key until the lock is completely locked.
- Thoroughly check the references of day care providers. Ensure they are licensed, screened by public safety, trained, and insured.
- Explore the school's policy for calling parents when children are absent or tardy, as well as the policy on children leaving school grounds with an adult other than a parent or guardian.
- Join the PTA or other parent–teacher organization.
- Keep a close watch on your children's moods and emotions. Talk to them about things that seem to be bothering them.
- If you feel that the school's security and safety measures are inadequate, work cooperatively with school officials, other parents, and local law enforcement agencies to improve the situation.
- Become a "Class Parent."
- Volunteer to help with an existing school accident, crime, fire prevention or safety program, or speak to your public safety agencies about beginning one. Mobilize other parents to participate.
- Get together with other community, civic, religious, and neighborhood groups and organize a community all-hazards mitigation

group to address local, state, and national school issues. New construction and capital improvements to proven practice specifications for seismic, severe weather, wild-fires or other regional and man-made disasters is a terrific starting point.

- Look at risk holistically with cross-functional subject matter experts to leverage tax dollars, foundation grants and volunteer resources.
- Establish safe places where children know they can go in case of danger on their way to and from school.
- Start an extended day care program for children of working parents with screened, trained and certified personnel.
- Encourage the integration of school safety and crime prevention information into the school's curriculum for all grades K through 12.

4.4 HOME ALONE: LATCHKEY CHILDREN

Children who are at home alone taking care of themselves for some part of the day are called latchkey children. Usually, parents are working and do not arrive home until after the children come home from school.

According to the crime prevention resources website for the city of Claremont, California, "children who are in a self-care situation are about three times more likely to be involved in accidents, engage in delinquent behavior, or be victimized than children supervised by adults."[3] Although parents cannot be with their children all of the time, there are steps that can help children prepare to cope with difficult situations. In addition, with help, children can be responsible for their own security when parents are not around.

4.4.1 What Parents Can Do

Parents are responsible for making sure that children are safe, secure, and well prepared to care for themselves. This includes:

- Setting a good example including regularly checking, recharging, or replenishing fire extinguishers, first aid kits, smoke detector or emergency radio batteries and other non perishable supplies.
- Teaching your children basic safety and security rules including your emergency plan.

[3]"Young Children at Home Alone," City of Claremont, accessed September 13, 2013, http://www.ci.claremont.ca.us/ps.crimeprevention.cfm?ID=1862.

- Knowing your children, where they are, and who they are with.
- Clearly communicating rules and limits. Work out rules for having friends over, for doing homework and completing household chores, for watching television, and so forth.
- Working with children to increase their level of responsibility and to improve their ability to make sound judgments. Children can build up their levels of competence and practical skills when they are home alone; being responsible can also increase their sense of confidence and self-esteem.
- Watching carefully to ensure that rules and procedures are being followed.
- Taking the time to lock up items that may be dangerous but about which children are naturally curious (such as guns, medicine, power tools, alcohol, and cleaning products) in a secure location that is out of sight.
- Letting them know that it is okay to share their fear or mistrust of people or situations and you will work with them to improve their and your confidence.

For more tips for parents of children who are home alone regularly and for the children themselves, the city of Claremont has an excellent list of guidance on its crime prevention website (mentioned earlier in this section). It includes information on promoting children's self-care skills, finding community resources, and following household routines.

4.5 SEXUAL ASSAULT

The most effective way to protect your children, from both sexual assault and other security risks, is to stay close and communicate well. Children who feel that no one is listening and that they have no one to talk to are more vulnerable to exploitation than children who feel closely connected.

Assault and sexual assault is a growing problem for parents and children. If your child is the victim of any crime, from bullying to sexual abuse, do not blame him or her. Listen and offer sympathy.

If a child has been sexually assaulted, or if you suspect that an assault has taken place, report it immediately to the police or to a child protection agency.

There are steps you can take to reduce your children's risk. This section covers these steps in three main areas:

1. What you can do to prevent sexual assault
2. Teaching children basic safety rules
3. How to detect sexual assault

4.5.1 What You Can Do to Prevent Sexual Assault
The most important step is establishing a relationship that helps your children feel comfortable talking about difficult things, such as someone inappropriately touching them, approaching them in an inappropriate manner, or making them feel uncomfortable. In addition:

- Know where your children are at all times. Be familiar with their care-givers, friends, their day-to-day activities, their bus drivers, clergy, scout leaders, teachers, and anyone else who regularly interacts with them.
- Teach your children to trust their own feelings. Let them know that they have the right to say "No" to whatever feels wrong and let you know about it.
- Be careful about baby-sitters, day care providers, and any other individual who has custody of your children. Conduct thorough reference checks on anyone or any group that will have responsible custody of your children. Require a public safety diligence check if one is available.
- Do not force children to hug, kiss, or sit on someone's lap if they do not want to. Allow children to control with whom they have close physical contact. This helps children understand that they have the right to refuse to engage in inappropriate touching, and that they are in control of their own bodies. Allow them to have their own personal space.

4.5.2 Teaching Children Basic Safety Rules
As soon as your children can talk, they can begin the process of learning how to protect themselves against sexual abuse. Teach your children:

- Not to get into a car or go anywhere with any person unless you have given specific permission;
- To stay away from strangers and from anyone who hangs around playgrounds, public restrooms, and schools;

- Never to keep a "special secret" from parents and teachers;
- Not to let someone take their picture without approval from parents or teachers;
- That no one should touch their private body parts; and
- To be assertive and say "No" to anyone who touches them inappropriately or who makes them feel uncomfortable.

4.5.3 How to Detect Sexual Assault

Sexual assault of children is often a repeat crime, with many children being victimized a number of times by the same offender.

Sexual assault often leaves children very confused and uncomfortable, and unwilling to talk to parents or teachers about what is happening. Encouraging your children to talk about experiences and feelings that make them and you feel uncomfortable is the key to protecting your children.

There are some consistent indicators that point to sexual abuse:

- Changes in behavior such as extreme mood swings, fearfulness, loss of appetite, sudden secretiveness, withdrawal from normal activities, refusal to go to school, unexplained hostility toward a baby-sitter or relative, an increase in anxiety, or excessive crying.
- Bed-wetting, nightmares, fear of going to bed, and other sleep disturbances.
- Acting out inappropriate sexual activity or showing an unusual interest in sexual matters.
- A sudden aggressiveness or other rebellious behavior.
- Regression to infantile behavior.
- Fear of certain places, people, or activities, especially the fear of being alone with certain people.
- Pain, itching, bleeding, fluid, bruises, or rawness in the genital area, or venereal disease.

4.6 SUICIDE

Suicide among young people is a serious problem. Fortunately, understanding the reasons behind suicide and recognizing the early-warning signs can help prevent it in most cases.

4.6.1 Suspected Causes of Suicide

No one can say for sure why a young person chooses to take his or her own life, but common causes include the following:

- Depression
- Family problems
- Family and friend suicide history or pacts
- A significant loss, such as the death of a close friend or relative
- Pressure to succeed
- Poor self-esteem
- Loneliness
- Illness, especially a prolonged illness
- Drug-related psychological problems
- A violent lifestyle
- Stress

4.6.2 Recognizing the Early Warning Signs

Suicide does not happen without a cause. By staying alert to the clues that someone may be considering suicide, you could prevent a suicide.

Some of the clues that may indicate a person is considering suicide include the following:

- A previous suicide attempt
- Telling people that he or she might commit suicide
- Depression, lack of interest, withdrawal from friends
- Themes of death recurring frequently in conversation or artwork
- Sudden, unexplained happiness
- Problems in school
- Giving away possessions, or indications that the person is putting his or her affairs in order
- Unusual acquisitions, purchases or thefts of weapons, rope, or medication
- Substance abuse
- Withdrawal from a normal routine

4.6.3 What You Can Do

If you feel that a child has attempted or may attempt suicide:

- Confer with a qualified mental health subject matter expert or seek a referral to one from a family physician or public health agency.

- Report your concerns or those of a teacher, care giver or other interested party that may have observed warning signs.
- Refer the child to someone who is experienced and qualified to help.
- Gather and read information on suicide from competent mental health providers and agencies.
- Talk with the child about your concerns.
- Recognize the early warning signs.

4.7 VANDALISM

Vandalism is a crime that hurts communities and costs money.

Vandalism takes many forms, including spray paint and other graffiti, knocked-over mailboxes and trash bins, broken trees and shrubs, missing traffic and street signs, destroyed books in libraries, broken lights and windows, damaged public telephones and playground equipment, as well as many other kinds of property defacement and destruction.

Most vandals are young people—grade schoolers, teens, and young adults—who destroy property because they are bored, angry, or want revenge.

Vandalism might be done to defy authority, to announce territorial rights, or to support a cause. Vandals often work in groups. Graffiti is typically used as part of a gang's tactics to take over a neighborhood. Individuals often engage in serial vandalism as a form a self promotion or guerilla art.

4.7.1 Vandalism Hurts Communities

Communities suffer from vandalism when it goes unchecked. It is often an early warning sign that crime is increasing in a neighborhood. People feel powerless when their property is destroyed and when their neighborhood looks blighted. Sometimes injuries occur or are made worse by vandalism, such as when accidents happen because traffic signs are missing or destroyed, or when someone cannot call police or 911 because a public phone has been broken.

4.7.2 Working to Prevent Vandalism

Vandalism can be reduced by citizens—both adults and young people—who get involved.

- Young people are a good source of energy for cleaning up graffiti and restoring property damaged by vandalism. When young people get involved, they can become part of the solution instead of being part of the problem.
- Clean up vandalism as soon as you see it. Repair broken playground equipment, remove graffiti, restore broken trees and shrubs, and replace missing signs. Do not allow gangs or other vandals to bring blight to your neighborhood.
- Report any act of vandalism to the police, school authorities, or your neighborhood homeowners association. Ask police or a city agency to set up a hot line for reporting vandalism.
- Adopt a street or a park, perhaps in cooperation with a community group, church, or business. Plant trees and bushes. Once each month, clean up the litter. Keep an eye on things in your adopted area.
- Work with neighborhood organizations to hold a "clean up your yard" event each year to help remove unwanted items and other garbage from the neighborhood. Some private contractors specialize in yard clean-ups and offer free assessments.
- Be certain that abandoned vehicles and large appliances that could endanger children (refrigerators etc.) are removed or dismantled. Confer with public agencies to see what services are provided.
- Keep a close watch on abandoned houses. Stay in close contact with city officials to make certain high risk abandoned structures are boarded, renovated or torn down.
- Work with your neighborhood groups to request more police patrols; especially bicycle or foot patrols. Seek information and training from your local police to begin your own neighborhood watch.
- Involve local businesses and young people in the painting of murals in places that are particularly susceptible to graffiti. Consider designating space for graffiti artists.
- Protect your house or apartment building with good locks and exterior lighting.

4.8 WEAPONS

As concern continues to grow about violence and the toll it is taking on our children and young people, it is important to remember that weapons are contributing to the problem.

Children should not have access to a weapon unless they are on a range or hunt with responsible adults who offer precautionary safety. Accidental gun deaths, homicides and suicides occur daily as a result of poor weapon security.

It is typically against the law for anyone under 18 years of age to possess in a public place any knife, dart, or other instrument that could be used for cutting or stabbing. It is also typically unlawful for a juvenile to carry any kind of pistol, including a spring gun, or a rubberband gun (zip gun) that shoots BBs, pellets, or other types of ammunition.

Although weapons of any kind are strictly prohibited in schools, students with weapons have become frequent problems. Increasingly, cities are declaring schools to be **drug-free** and **gun-free** zones, which then allows stiffer penalties to be imposed on those who violate existing laws.

As a parent, you can help reduce the availability of weapons by supporting strict gun safety regulations. You can also help by setting a good example and by turning off the violence. Help your child find alternatives to the violent TV shows, video games, and movies that are commonplace entertainment.

Teach your children to avoid people and situations that can lead to violence. This includes avoiding alcohol and drugs, as well as learning conflict resolution without resorting to violence. **"Use your words."** Avoiding places where confrontation and fighting often occurs or leaving a situation where it is evolving are two proven tactics for personal safety.

For more information, see Chapter 2: Personal Protection.

4.9 DRUGS

The first step in preventing abuse is to reduce the use of alcohol and drugs among both children and adults, since children emulate the behaviors they see. Research shows that the main reason that kids don't use alcohol, tobacco, or drugs is because of positive parental influence.

Alcohol, tobacco, and drug use amongst children is not only unlawful, it is unacceptable. The public health consequences are enormous. Soft drug experimentation at an early age, along with genetic predispositions, arguably places children at greater risk for more addictive drugs, such as cocaine, crack, and heroin, as well as other pharmaceutical stimulants and depressants.

Addictive risks include hazards ranging from criminal violence to unsafe sex. Drug dealing is big business. Individual lives, family welfare, and communities are put at risk.

Controlling or reducing the drug problem involves working with children and adults to reduce the likelihood that they will become users. Prescription drugs should be secured. Awareness and reporting of high risk behaviors should be encouraged. Taking steps to reduce the opportunities for drug dealers follows.

4.9.1 Working with Children

Working with children requires that you communicate the facts in a way that makes a lasting impression. Teachable moments include your setting a good example by controlling drinking, ensuring designated drivers, and cleaning out dated prescriptions from the medicine cabinet. Family involvement in volunteer neighborhood groups and programs can help in many ways.

Drug use and drug-related crime is often connected to other problems, such as a lack of stability and safety at home, examples set by adults and older children. Sometimes the best way to attack drug use is to work first on the related problems. Open communications by caring family members and neighbors help.

Our own lack of awareness, supervision, or carelessness often enables avoidable abuse. The presumption of benefits, including getting buzzed, high, or just relaxing, can be attractive with no down side. We must be more engaged to make a difference.

4.9.2 Communicating the Facts

The most important fact to communicate to your children is that you value their health, well-being, special qualities, and unique potential. Make it clear that drug use may diminish their ability to assess risks. The more you value your children, the more likely they will hold themselves in high esteem.

- Drugs may particularly harm youngsters. Unchecked drug use can have serious physical and psychological consequences. High morbidity accident rates alone are concerning. Risks associated with teen pregnancy, HIV, and other transmittable diseases are well documented.

- Additional impairment of intellectual or physical development may put a child's education and health at risk, which impacts future earning potential.
- Drug use is not acceptable. It is against the law. Drug-related crime is the cause of a great deal of violence and loss. Drugs get people into trouble and sometimes get killed.
- There are positive, drug-free alternatives. Help your children explore these alternatives, such as sports, reading, camping, hiking, games, music, or art.
- Every person has the right to say "No." Each person is ultimately responsible for himself or herself. Everyone has the right to not be pressured into doing something that puts them and others at risk.
- People in general, and particulary children, do as others do. Therefore, it is important for adults to model behaviors. Tell. Show. Do. Take an interest and participate in fun activities and demonstrate responsible behavior with any risk.

4.9.3 Using Teachable Moments

Children retain very little information and rarely change their attitudes and behaviors when adults lecture them on a subject, especially one as complex and difficult as drug use.

Look for teachable moments in which to reach children:

- When watching a movie or television show
- When something happens to someone in the family, at their school, or in the community
- When they ask you a question directly or indirectly related to drugs
- When you read or hear a news story about someone whom they might consider to be a hero or leader, such as a sports figure or an entertainment figure, who has been involved with drugs or taken a stand against drugs

When you have an opportunity to discuss drugs:

- Talk calmly, openly, and without anger. Be honest. Talk about your own experiences and near misses or those of others factually.
- Be certain that you tell your children, in clear and simple terms, that drug use is unacceptable. It is illegal, dangerous, and ruins lives.

- Discuss the subject matter, not the personalities involved. Challenging children's motives or the appropriateness of their current friends might cause defensive or defiant behavior.
- Know the facts, but do not exaggerate. It is easy to lose credibility with children.
- Talk face to face, in person. Be an active listener. Let your children talk about their knowledge, experiences, and fears or concerns about drugs.
- Maintain an ongoing dialogue. Try to cover one point in a discussion. Use another discussion to talk about another point. Let your children know that you are engaged and will stay engaged in the discussion.
- Remember that you set the example. Your children will compare your actions with your words and will be guided accordingly. If you have made a mistake, apologize and move on. Do not become angry or defensive.

4.9.4 Drug Checklist for Children

Do not delay talking to your children about drugs. And don't expect schools to do it all. Children need to see that their parents are involved.

- Start your children on a drug education program through your school or community group.
- Make sure children understand the difference between prescriptions and legal medications and street drugs.
- Use the common street names for street drugs when identifying them to your children.
- Explain the hazards and bad side-effects as a consequence of using street drugs.
- Explain why some people use drugs and the problems they have.
- Teach children to say **No** to drugs by using role-playing.
- Tell your children never to use any drugs without your permission.

4.9.5 Signs that a Child May Be Using Drugs

By knowing the signs that indicate possible drug use, you may be able to help prevent further use.

- Do your child's moods or activity level change quickly? Drugs can cause a person to become more irritable, secretive, withdrawn, angry, or very happy without any apparent cause.

- Has your child become less responsible? Does he or she have difficulty remembering things? You might notice your child coming home late from school or other events, failing to do chores or homework, or becoming dishonest.
- Is your child changing friends or changing lifestyles? You might notice that your child has new interests, has unexplained amounts of cash, or starts to dress and act very differently.
- Is it difficult to communicate with your child? Does he or she avoid talking to you face to face and find it uncomfortable to be around the family?
- Does your child show physical deterioration? Is he or she losing interest in personal appearance or have a generally unhealthy appearance? Gaining or losing weight rapidly? Having difficulty concentrating?

4.9.6 Reducing Drugs in Your Community
Neighborhoods across the country have successfully used a coordinated approach to reducing drugs in their community.

- Ask public health and safety professionals for guidance in forming a neighborhood group that walks the neighborhood and discreetly records, photographs, or videos, and communicates license plate numbers and descriptions of known and suspected drug dealers.
- Use discretion and good judgment when faced with problems of drug use or sales or other criminal activity in your neighborhood. Think about how you can report a drug problem without opening yourself up to the possibility of retaliation. It is important to report crimes, but it is equally important to remain safe. Explore anonymous crime reporting programes like CrimeStoppers.
- Refrain from doing business with restaurants, bars, landlords, and others who choose to ignore drug dealers.
- Organize community clean-up campaigns with professional public health care guidance to remove drug paraphernalia and litter from the streets, paint over graffiti, plant flowers and trees, and repair broken items. Show people that your community cares about its appearance and that it is not helpless in the face of crime.
- Plan and develop a drug-free school zone with the cooperative efforts of public safety agencies, parents, youth organizations, and school officials.
- A drug-free school zone provides a solid framework on which to build a community-wide commitment to reducing drug use. Expand

the boundaries of the zone to include other areas that have drug-related problems.

- Drug dealers often use run-down or abandoned buildings. Ask fire, health, and housing agencies to inspect these buildings for code violations and to shut down these hazardous properties. Urge your city officials to tear down abandoned buildings or to sell them through civic programs for rehabilitation.
- Ask the police for more patrols. Perhaps a mini-station can be opened in your area.
- Ascertain preferred communications for public safety organizations.
- Use the law to make life difficult for drug dealers. Property owners can give police permission to enter private property such as parking lots and outside stairs to investigate and prosecute trespassers and loiterers. Landlords can require diligent background check of renters and re-write their leases to specifically bar criminal activity.
- Asset forfeiture laws, nuisance abatement laws, and drug-free zone laws can all be used to seize assets from convicted drug dealers; to bring suits against property owners who tolerate drugs, graffiti, and litter; and to increase the penalties for drug-related activities on school property.
- Contact your local prosecutor's office for help and information about your lawful rights and obligations.
- Find out who is responsible for towing abandoned cars in your area. Be persistent about reporting these cars until they are removed.
- Telephone companies can fix pay phones so that only outgoing calls are possible. Public utilities can shut off service to buildings that are being used for illegal activities.
- Organize a Neighborhood Watch program. Post large, colorful notices that people are watching and reporting drug-related activities and other crimes.
- Get young people involved in all of your community's anti-drug activities. Make them part of the neighborhood improvement team, and let them contribute their energy and good ideas to the effort.

4.10 AWAY AT COLLEGE

When your daughter or son is choosing a school, make inquiries regarding the institution's public safety record. Ascertain the size and professional capabilities of the campus public safety organizations.

Most colleges offer parent–student orientations that can answer your questions and prepare both of you for new risks. Ensure your student is aware and engaged for their own safety. Equip them with a mobile smart phone with an app that will allow them to summon help and communicate their GPS location.

4.10.1 What Your Daughter or Son Should Know

Many of the personal security issues at college are similar to the ones faced by all adults. See the following chapters for help:

- Chapter 2: Personal Protection
- Chapter 3: Assault and Sexual Assault
- Chapter 5: Home Safety and Security
- Chapter 8: Automobiles

The school public health and safety policies, procedures and services should be suffiently robust to mitigate all-hazards risk. Impress on your child the value of their own awareness and engagement of services that may make the difference for a successful education.

4.10.2 College Policies and Services

Most colleges have security- and safety-related policies and services, including:

- access control;
- escort services;
- crime prevention and public safety alerts;
- emergency communications and guidelines;
- criminal and unethical conduct governance;
- investigative and disciplinary procedures;
- housing assistance;
- dormitory resident assistance programs;
- counseling services;
- medical services; and
- curricula, speakers, and special topic presentations that address current risk issues.

4.10.3 What You Can Do

As a parent, you should become a student of campus security and safety issues. Determine the school's assets for all-hazards risk mitigation. You can spend time with your children on campus, and join volunteer and advisory efforts to reduce personal security and safety risks. Most of all, you can teach your children to adhere to the following guidelines:

- Be personally responsible and avoid situations that they sense are dangerous.
- Be aware, alert and equipped for documenting and reporting high risk events and conditions.
- Behave appropriately during times of risk.
- Stay current with risk incidents and trends on campus.
- Report incidents and take action as soon as it is safe to do so.
- Respect the rights of others.
- Contribute positively to the community.

4.11 GANGS

Communities experience various levels of gang activity and gang problems. Gangs invariably have a detrimental effect on community safety. Subcultures of criminal and antisocial behavior, drug use, and vandalism often cause violence. People, young and old, face intimidation in their homes, neighborhoods, recreational areas, schools, and workplaces. The negative impact on young people is serious, as generations may be drawn into a violent and antisocial lifestyle.

4.11.1 General Characteristics

Gang members are typically concerned with dominating a territory, making a profit, and promoting their own reputation.

- Gangs attempt to manipulate their environment, using force and intimidation, to meet their needs.
- Most active gang members are between the ages of 13 and 21, though there are also younger and older gang members. Gangs include both males and females.
- The hard-core elements of gangs have little interest in acting responsibly, show a lack of compassion and remorse, tend to be calloused, show contempt for authority figures, and have trouble controlling their impulses.
- Many gangs are involved in extortion and trafficking of drugs and stolen property.

- Gangs often mark out a certain neighborhood as their territory or turf. Graffiti is used to identify a gang's territory and challenge other gangs. Graffiti means something, and it can often be interpreted by public safety subject matter experts.

4.11.2 Why Young People Join Gangs

Although there are differences between individuals, many young people join gangs for one or more of the following reasons.

- Gang involvement may be an attempt to be protected and to survive in a very violent environment.
- Young people are looking for a family-like social group to which they can belong.
- In many communities, there is a lack of productive school and extracurricular activities.
- They may be influenced by parent or sibling involvement in a gang.
- They may be seeking thrills and excitement.
- They may be searching for an identity or self-esteem, or seeking status and power.
- Gangs can offer financial opportunities where legitimate jobs are few and far between.
- Gangs might have ethnic or philosophical attractiveness for some young people.

4.11.3 How to Identify Gangs and Gang Activity

Most gang members are proud of their gangs and freely admit that they are members. Members on the fringe of the gang may not openly admit they are members, but will often state that their friends are.

- Gang activity is not confined to the disadvantaged minority youth in the inner cities. Gangs find their members from every race, social class, and lifestyle.
- Members openly display tattoos and dress in a style or color that identifies their particular gang. Hand signs, phrases and symbols distinguish affiliations.
- Graffiti is one of the most visible signs of gangs. Groups of young people wearing distinguishable clothing is another.
- Excessive gang activity at night is common. Alcohol, drugs, and violence are often routine.

- Excessive vandalism, harassment and extortion complaints are signs that gang activity is increasing.
- Drive-by shootings are often gang related.

4.11.4 What You Can Do
Becoming involved in your community organizations is the best way to reduce gang activity and the impact it has on your neighborhood.

- Reduce the opportunities for crime.
- Work with local public safety, Boys and Girls Clubs, churches, scouting, sports programs, etc. to keep kids involved in activities that have a positive influence.
- Watch for early signs of problems.
- Actively promote awareness of personal security issues.
- Report developing high-risk conditions that make you afraid for your own safety or that of others.

See the section *Crime Prevention* and Hazard Mitigation in Chapter 1: Preventing and Reporting High Risk Events for more information.

CHAPTER 5

Home Safety and Security

5.1 OVERVIEW

Although you cannot ever make your home completely safe and secure against manmade and natural hazards, you can greatly reduce your chances of becoming a victim. There are several proactive steps you can take to make sure your family home is adequately protected.

Review your home's overall physical safety and security profile and take a close look at how well your family follows precautionary prevention and emergency procedures. Good safety and security habits are just as important as physical improvements.

5.2 HOME SAFETY AND SECURITY SURVEY

Family and personal safety are usually the most important reasons for all-hazards awareness and mitigation efforts. Asset security typically is a close second, including our residences and all valued possessions and protected information therein. Most homes and apartments are vulnerable to manmade (accidents and crimes) and natural hazards (seismic, severe weather, etc.).

The good news is that most home injuries and asset losses are preventable. Others are mitigable as you lessen consequences. First and foremost, be informed. Research the historical risks for your community and neighborhood. Check crime, flood, seismic, and storm history before you invest and make sure insurance is available. Home owner or renter insurance covers most hazards but there may be exclusions. Insurance companies may also provide resources for risk reduction planning like accident, crime and fire prevention.

If earthquakes, floods, hurricanes, tornados, or wild fires are a possibility, reliable emergency communications for public safety advisories including evacuation and shelter-in-place are a must. Our ability to plan ahead is valuable. It is not hard to anticipate hazards of the past revisiting in the future.

Fault lines shift. Lightning strikes. Winds blow. People play with fire. If a criminal really wants to break in, chances are that he or she will be successful. Your job is to be aware, equipped, and informed in time to prevent or avoid the harshest consequences of risk.

- Develop good security and safety habits. Lock your doors and windows even when you are home.
- Keep important papers, emergency cash, weapons or ammunition in fire-rated security containers.
- Provision water and nonperishable foods for a manmade or natural catastrophic event. Your ability to shelter-in-place or evacuate as instructed by public safety is consequential.
- Make certain laptops and portable communications devices are logged for insurance coverage, password-protected, patched and backed-up.
- Consider "find me" or remote hard drive destruction software.
- Investigate motion detection lighting inside and outside your home to prevent accidents, alert you or your neighbors to trespass. These devices save energy, provide just-in-time lighting and contain costs for running your household.
- Equip your living space with duress intrusion, smoke, carbon monoxide, radon or other risk detection devices for local alarm and/or remote monitoring.
- Emergency preparedness may include designating an interior safe room with fortified construction, a security/fire rated door, communications, provisions and generator or battery back-up.
- Train for emergencies with licensed, certified instructors.
- Emergency equipment and supplies (first aid kits, fire extinguishers, flashlights, detectors) require inspection, reprovisioning, and recharging on an annual basis.

- When you travel for business or go on vacation, do not make the information public. Only notify need-to-know, trusted persons of your itinerary. Arrange for mail or newspaper delivery suspension.
- Leave a voicemail or out-of-office instructions that you will be unavailable and designate others for urgent communications.
- Begin your security and safety check with the front door and work clockwise around the entire outside of your home. Include all doors and windows, finishing with the back yard, fence and shrubs, gates, and garage.
- Make certain a "go bag" (think wheeled luggage) with absolute essentials is stored in a hallway or closet.
- Shrubbery should never allow hiding places or block the view of your doors or windows. Low profile thorny bushes, transparent fencing, and civilly worded signage can communicate defensible space without being inhospitable to invited guests.
- House or building numbers should be clearly visible from the street. Illuminated numbers are a good idea for both the front and back of the house. This helps police emergency first responders find your home. Urge your neighbors to display their house numbers clearly, too.
- A wide-angle viewer lets you identify a visitor before you open the door. A minimum of 180 degrees visibility in a viewer is recommended.
- Make your home appear occupied at all times. The use of timers or motion units to turn lights, radios, or televisions on and off in different rooms at different times can discourage many criminals.
- Lock your doors and windows. Most intruders do not pick locks, since the time it takes to do so increases their chances of being discovered.
- Be certain that you have a bedroom door that can be locked. You should also have a telephone in the room in case of an emergency.
- Make a point to notice vehicles and people you have not seen before in your neighborhood.
- Get to know your neighbors. Participate in or establish a Neighborhood Watch program. Many burglars say that neighbors who look around and are aware of what is going on in their neighborhood are a great deterrent.
- Always change the locks when you move into a new residence. You never know who else may still have a key. Replace all door strike plates with ones that provide for a hardened core steel rod connected to the strike plate to protrude through the doorjamb and into

the framing studs. Use three-inch hardened wood screws to secure the locking mechanism and strike plate to the door and door frame.
- Work with your landlord or condominium association and neighbors for a building or community risk assessment. Public safety professionals are often available to brief interested groups.

5.3 DOORS AND WINDOWS

Minimum home security requires that you take steps to keep intruders from entering your home through any door or window, unless they resort to using destructive force.

Doors and windows that are not locked or that are inadequately secured can provide easy access to your home. Most intruders enter through unlocked doors and windows. Criminals are far less likely to enter your home if access is difficult, visible, noisy, and time-consuming.

When evaluating your home's physical security, take into account all the different types of doors and windows on the property.

- Wood and metal doors
- Door hinge protection
- Sliding doors
- Inactive doors
- Window locks and latches
- Sliding windows
- Double hung windows
- Casement windows
- Iron grilles and burglar bars

5.3.1 Wood and Metal Doors
- The best exterior doors are metal or solid-core hardwood, at least 1¾″ thick.
- Make sure every door to the outside has a dead bolt lock with a minimum 1½″ bolt.
- Do not use thumb latch dead bolt locks on doors where the latch is easily accessible through a side panel window.
- Check that lock assemblies on all exterior doors with doorknobs have an anti-friction tongue as a standard. This is extremely important for door locks that do not have dead bolts.

- Do not leave keys in a double-sided keyway dead bolt when the dead bolt is accessible through a side panel window.

5.3.2 Door Hinge Protection

If your home has hinged exterior doors that open outward, the hinge pins are on the outside of the home and vulnerable to attack. To protect your door from being lifted from its hinges, follow the simple steps outlined below.

If your door swings out to open, and it has standard duty hinges without locking screws to secure the pins, the following safety measures are recommended:

a. Drill two holes opposite each other in the center of both hinge plate leaves.
b. Drive a headless screw or nail into the hole on the door frame side of the hinge plate. Leave a half inch of the screw or nail protruding so that it enters the opposite hole when the door is closed.
c. Repeat this process for every hinge on the door. Even if the pins are removed, the door still cannot be taken off its hinges.

5.3.3 Sliding Doors

Secure sliding doors to keep them from being pushed open or from being pried up and out of the track. A simple way to secure an inside sliding door is to drill a downward sloping hole through the top channel into the top portion of the sliding door frame and insert a pin into the hole.

Sticks or bars may be placed at the bottom of the doorjamb to secure a sliding door, but these can sometimes be forced out of the way. Installing a slide bolt provides minimum security for a sliding door. For additional security, add a key-operated padlock or dead bolt.

5.3.4 Inactive Doors

Install flush bolts at the top and bottom of an inactive door. Flush bolts stop an intruder from tampering with them if the doors are locked.

5.3.5 Window Locks and Latches

Windows should be secured to eliminate the chance of someone prying them open. Most intruders will avoid breaking glass because it attracts attention. Window locks, used with other security measures such as good lighting, provide a good deterrent. Lock your windows when you go out, even if you plan to be out for only a few minutes.

- Most windows have latches, although many window latches do not provide ideal security. Provide your windows with additional protection such as a barrel bolt lock. Or, drill small holes in the window frame where the top and bottom windows overlap and insert nails in these holes.
- Make sure all windows, frames, and locks are in good condition.
- When special equipment is used for securing windows, make sure that these devices comply with fire codes and that everyone knows how to use them properly.

Warning: Leave one window in the bedroom on the ground floor and one window on the second floor available as fire exits.

5.3.6 Sliding Windows
Secure a sliding window by placing a rod or dowel in the sliding track. Most locksmiths and hardware stores sell screw-controlled anti-burglary clamps. These devices are placed in the tracks of windows and sliding glass doors to prevent them from sliding open.

5.3.7 Double Hung Windows
Double hung window latches may be pried open. If the window is not used, screw it shut. For double hung windows being used, drill a downward sloping hole into the top of the bottom window, through and into the bottom of the top window. Insert a pin or nail.

5.3.8 Casement Windows
Casement windows are generally secure in themselves. Be certain that the latch works properly and that the operator has no excess play in it. If it does, replace the worn hardware. For added security, simply remove the operator from all windows and keep one in a safe place by each room.

5.3.9 Iron Grilles and Burglar Bars
Decorative iron grilles for ground-level entrances and windows provide additional security for windows. Due to the danger of fire, decorative iron grilles are not recommended for bedroom windows unless they can be opened from the inside.

If burglar bars are used, they should be installed to hinge outward from the window or door and secured with a double cylinder dead bolt lock. This allows you to exit the window or door in case of emergency.

5.3.10 Alarm Systems

The design and installation of an alarm system for your residence should be performed by a security professional.

- Premises signs and window decals are excellent psychological deterrents to the casual intruder.
- Have a strobe light installed at the corner of your residence nearest to the street. The light should be wired to activate when the alarm system is activated. This will help emergency responders.
- Consider the value of security- and safety-equipped residences and the proximity of first responders when searching for a new residence.

5.4 EXTERIOR

A residence that is clearly visible to neighbors and the street discourages the potential intruder. Use at least standard lighting levels in your doorways and driveways. You may wish to add motion detection lighting in back of or at the corners. If possible, place lights high enough to prevent tampering.

- Trim shrubs so that windows and doors are in full view from the street. Unobstructed doors and windows are a deterrent because the intruder is forced to work in the open where detection is likely.
- Maintain adequate lighting, especially at vulnerable entry points. Some power companies will install a yard light for a reasonable monthly charge.
- Do not leave ladders and tools outside where burglars can use them to enter your home.
- Expensive equipment and bicycles should be secured when not in use.
- Always keep garage doors locked. CCTV and access control are recommended for multi-dwelling residential buildings.
- Do not hide keys outside your residence. Most hiding spots are relatively obvious and burglars can easily discover them. Invest in a lockbox that can enable first responder access.
- Get a mailbox that is large enough to totally conceal mail, or install a small mail slot in your door that prevents access.

- Do not reveal unnecessary personal information on your mailbox or doorbell. For example, use *M. Jones* instead of *Mary Jones*.

5.4.1 Garage Security

Failure to close and lock garage doors presents a serious security problem. Even when garage doors are locked, their locks can often be defeated. Multi-dwelling garages should ideally feature access control equipped with closed circuit television or duress alarm.

- If your overhead garage door rolls on tracks, drill a hole in the track large enough for the shackle of the padlock. Place the padlock through the track hole so it acts as a brace against the door being opened. Steel pins can be used in place of the padlock.
- The door leading from your attached garage into your house should have a dead bolt lock mounted on it. If intruders gain entrance to the garage, they are concealed and might find the tools necessary to continue the entry and burglary of your home.
- When arriving home, be certain that the garage door is completely closed before unlocking the car doors and getting out.
- Electronic garage door openers with automatic locking devices offer good security against burglaries. Always keep the transmitter box that activates these openers in a safe place. It can be stolen and used by a burglar to open your garage door.
- If you suspect that a stranger has discovered the frequency that activates your opener, contact a dealer who sells openers to change the frequency. When on vacation, unplug the transmitter box to safeguard against the garage door being opened by an intruder.
- If you are leaving your home for an extended period of time, locking your garage door from the interior is recommended for additional security.
- Place translucent contact paper or curtains over garage windows. Install a yard light that can be turned on from inside the garage. A well-lighted yard offers security as you go from garage to house at night. You should also be able to turn the yard light on from inside the house.

5.4.2 Checklist for Garage Security

✓ Always close and lock garage doors.
✓ Consider using an automatic garage door opener.
✓ Do not leave the garage door opener in plain sight inside your vehicle. If your vehicle is stolen, the thief now has your address

from the insurance papers in the car, the garage door opener, and possibly a spare key to your home.

✓ Consider the door leading from the house to the garage as an exterior door. Install a metal or solid-core hardwood door 1¾″ thick.

✓ Install a viewer with at least 180 degrees of visibility in the door leading into your garage.

✓ When taking a trip, secure your garage by placing a common bicycle lock in the garage door track. This will prohibit opening the door from the outside.

5.5 OPERATION IDENTIFICATION

The Operation Identification burglary prevention program is an excellent resource for recovering lost and stolen property. Visit their website at http://www.opid.org/.

- Mark and photograph all high-value portable property with an identifying mark, such as your state and driver's license number (CA-B1234567). Never use your social security number. Your local public safety department may offer advice on engraving tools or permanent markers to identify your property.
- Make a record of all marked property and keep it in a safety deposit box or other safe location away from valuables. The record should include the identifying mark as well as descriptions and serial numbers of marked items. This information helps you identify stolen property quickly and make it more recoverable.
- Put Operation Identification stickers on windows near the front and back doors of your home. They tell a burglar that property is identified as yours and will be hard to sell to a dealer of stolen goods. (No dealer wants to be arrested with stolen articles, especially if they are easy to trace and identify.) You can get the stickers from your police department.
- Operation Identification numbers, when in the possession of someone other than the owner, can be used as evidence in court.

5.6 NEIGHBORHOOD WATCH

Block Watch clubs and Neighborhood Watch programs can help to reduce high-risk conditions including crime in your neighborhood.

Neighbors watch for emergencies and unusual behaviors and report them to each other and designated public safety agencies.

Block Watchers are trained by public safety professionals to identify and report suspicious, criminal, or high-risk behaviors and conditions. Neighborhood Watch is similar to Block Watch, but it may also implement a complete program of home security surveys and Operation Identification. To organize a Block Watch club or a Neighborhood Watch program, contact your police department. A crime prevention officer will meet with you and your neighbors to discuss these concepts in detail.

5.6.1 What to Do to Establish a Network

- Get to know your neighbors and become familiar with their routines. You are going to be partners in watching the activities on your block. Neighbors who look out for each other are the best front-line defense.
- Be observant. Report unusual or suspicious behavior or high risk conditions to local public safety agencies. If suspected criminal activity is observed and it is safe to do so, record, photograph, or write down descriptions of the person(s) and license numbers of any vehicles involved.
- Establish a meeting time and place convenient to all your neighbors.
- Exchange names and contact information with others.
- Above all, be concerned. It is the most effective way to prevent, reduce or mitigate risk and make your neighborhood safe.

5.6.2 Once the Network is Established

- Keep a trusted neighbor informed if your house is unoccupied for an extended period. It is important to leave your neighbor a way of reaching you if an emergency arises.
- Look after your neighbor's house when your neighbor is away, and ask your neighbor to look after yours. This includes collecting mail, newspapers, and other deliveries.
- Establish and attend regular neighborhood meetings with your local crime prevention officer. Find out about local crime trends and what you can do to improve them.
- Post Neighborhood Watch and Block Watch signs to let everyone know that your neighborhood is organized to fight crime and promote safety.

CHAPTER 6

Workplace Safety and Security

6.1 OVERVIEW

You can help make any workplace more safe and secure by following good practices and by encouraging others to be aware, detect, report, and mitigate high risk conditions. Knowing routine crime prevention, reporting, and emergency response procedures in advance can leave a caring impression with clients, customers, and visitors. More importantly, proactive measures can mitigate more serious injury and asset loss outcomes.

Introduce meetings with an overview of emergency procedures, including shelter in place or evacuation options. Point out emergency exits and shelter areas along with the usual orientation for bathrooms, coffee, and snack stations, particularly if you are in a high-risk, severe weather, or seismic-prone location. Security and safety reporting instructions on the back of your access or visitor badge can be an excellent means of communicating need-to-know information.

6.2 RISK MITIGATION

Many crimes and hazards cannot be prevented, even on the job where there are organized safety and security resources. Personal engagement is highly recommended to protect yourself and others. Some of the ways to avoid injury or mitigate unnecessary losses include the following:

- Orient yourself to your surrounding, and be familiar with emergency procedures and emergency reporting options.
- Take first aid and emergency community responder training.
- Secure your valuables in a location you can lock, or leave them at home.
- Backup and protect your personal information in accordance with your IT department's policies.
- Keep a log of company property you have in your possession.

6.2.1 Keep Your Valuables With You

Keep your purse, wallet, or other valuable items with you at all times, or keep them locked in a drawer, closet, desk, cabinet, or other locking device. Do not leave your purse on a desk. Do not leave your wallet in a jacket that is hanging on a chair or coat rack. Do not bring large amounts of cash to work.

If you bring any personal items to work, such as a coffee pot, a radio, or a calculator, identify them with your name and an identification number.

6.2.2 Check the Access Permission of Strangers

If you see someone who is not regularly in your area, offer assistance. If he or she does not have the proper escort or visitor badge, offer to help them get proper credentials at reception. Individuals who over-react or suspiciously decline your assistance should be discreetly reported to security or management.

If someone you do not know asks for confidential information or requests access to a restricted area, ask that person for identification. If you are not satisfied with the person's identification, ask your manager for assistance or contact security.

6.2.3 Report Any Person or Vehicle that Seems Suspicious

If you notice any condition (a propped open or unlocked security door), person (someone looking lost or looking around, carrying a duffel bag, etc.), or vehicle (idling in a parking lot or adjacent street) that seems suspicious, contact security or the appropriate public safety agency to request a patrol check. Suspicious behavior is anything that makes you feel afraid or uncomfortable.

6.2.4 Keep a Log of Company Property

Keep a log of the company property for which you are responsible, and be certain that it stays up-to-date. Store the list in a safe place (not in your desk) for future reference. Use a system of property passes to account for company property that leaves the building or is removed from its normal location for business purposes.

6.2.5 Report Company and Personal Property Losses Promptly

If you notice any property loss, whether it is company property or personal property, report the loss promptly to your supervisor, manager, security, or your local public safety agency. Use your property log to identify what is missing.

6.2.6 Model Security and Safety Behaviors

Engaged leaders model organizational proven practice behaviors. They lead by example, demonstrate team play, and care for their clients, colleagues, and customers. They abide by governance standards from access control and authorized use guidelines, ethical conduct, and risk reporting duties. They lead with courage when newer data for evolving risk conditions and mitigation opportunities demand change.

6.3 INAPPROPRIATE COMMUNICATIONS

Known and unknown persons can use phone, email, or other messaging communications to harass you and upset you. They also can attempt to collect information that might help harm you or others. Inappropriate communications may be criminal, especially when their intent is to defraud, extort, harass, or intimidate.

If you receive an inappropriate communication that concerns, upsets, or makes you afraid, report it immediately. Do not discard inappropriate emails, call logs, letters, gifts, messages, or voicemails–even if they are embarassing. All are considered evidence when investigating policy infractions and crimes. Skilled forensic investigators can often identify the sender even when he or she is anonymous or unknown to you.

6.3.1 If You Speak to a Harassing or Suspect Communicator

- Record the details (date, time, who, what, why, and where).
- Note any witnesses.
- If the communication is made by phone, note any background noise or conversation.
- Not any particulars of voice, accent, manner, or other peculiarities.
- Ask yourself: Is the caller's voice familiar? Did the voice sound disguised? Did the caller seem to know your schedule?

6.3.2 If You Receive a Communication with an Unusual Information Request

- Avoid providing any personal or company information before making certain that the request is legitimate.
- If the request is made by phone, ask the caller to send you the details of his or her request by email.
- Forward any suspicious letters or emails to management
- Never click hyperlinks from unknown persons, agencies, or organizations, as the link could introduce malware to your network.

6.4 WORKING BEFORE AND AFTER BUSINESS HOURS OR ON ASSIGNMENT

If you work before or after normal business hours, you can increase your security by following some basic procedures:

- Make arrangements in advance to arrive and leave work with someone else.
- Use escort services or valet parking if available.
- Keep emergency numbers near your phone.
- Notify security of any person, condition, or vehicle that seems suspicious.
- Ensure the building has minimum safety and security safeguards.

6.4.1 Arrive and Leave Work with Someone Else

If you are working late or coming in early, or when you're on assignment, try to meet another employee and arrive and/or leave together. If you are the only person in your office, check with neighboring businesses for someone else with a schedule like yours.

If you use public transportation, be certain you have up-to-date schedules. Check the safety and security record of any transportation provider. Try to avoid spending unnecessary time at a bus stop or other public transportation point, and only use recommended taxis or car services.

6.4.2 Ensure Your Work Area is Safe and Secure
Be aware of the minimum safety and security requirements for your work area. Request an orientation if one is not offered for access control, alarms, emergency reporting, evacuation, and shelter-in-place options, fire extinguishers, first aid kits, security services, etc.

6.4.3 Program Emergency Numbers and Capabilities on Your Phone
Keep emergency numbers for security, police, and fire (911) near your phone for quick access. Include your "in case of emergency" (ICE) contact as well as roadside assistance. Explore emergency assistance smartphone apps that will provide your status and GPS location to others.

6.5 PARKING YOUR CAR

As you go to and return from work, pay particular attention to how you park your car. This is especially true if you work before and after business hours. See Chapter 8: Automobiles for more information.

The basic principles for parking your car include the following:

- Park in a well-lighted place.
- Always lock your car and alarm it.
- Secure your valuables.
- Know how to approach and leave your car.

6.5.1 Park in a Well-Lighted Place
If possible, park in a well-lighted, well-traveled area within view of a camera. If you know you are going to be staying late, park your car under or near a light in the morning. If there are no spaces near lights when you arrive, move your car to a better location during the day.

6.5.2 Use an Escort Service if One is Available
If you work late, ask your security department or someone else (such as a coworker, a supervisor, or security personnel) to escort you to the parking lot.

6.5.3 Always Lock Your Car

Always lock and alarm your car and roll the windows up all the way when you park your car. If you notice strangers lurking in the parking lot, notify management, security, or the police right away.

6.5.4 Secure Your Valuables

Be certain that there are no valuable items in plain view inside your car. Either leave your valuables at home or lock them in the trunk before you leave your house. Transferring valuables to the trunk in plain view may invite unwanted attention and consequences.

6.5.5 Know How to Approach and Leave Your Car

As you approach your car, have your key in your hand and ready. Look under the car when you are still a safe distance away. When you get to your car, check both the back and front seats, and the floor, before you get in. Be wary of any vans that are parked near your car.

Look around your car before you get out. Do not unlock the doors until your seatbelt is off and you are ready to leave.

CHAPTER 7

When You Travel

7.1 OVERVIEW

Traveling, whether abroad or in the United States, for either business or pleasure, can be an enriching experience. It also presents some personal security risks that are out of the ordinary. To help you prepare for these risks, this chapter provides information on good travel security practices in seven main areas:

1. Planning your trip
2. Automobiles
3. Hotel security
4. Airports
5. International travel
6. Visiting the United States
7. Preparing to live outside the United States

7.2 PLANNING YOUR TRIP

The best way to protect yourself when you travel is to plan your trip ahead of time. Keep in mind that when you travel to unfamiliar places, you are more likely to feel disoriented. Make inquiries regarding trip insurance, route conditions, safety, security, weather, or special risk conditions at your destination(s). These will inform additional considerations for inoculation, trip insurance, and risk mitigation.

Carry a copy of your license, passport, and emergency contacts with you separate from other valuables that may be stolen. Check out smartphone apps that may show your security and safety status and alert local authorities to your location. Execute a power of attorney with a trusted family member who should have access to your bank accounts, insurance policies, or other resources if you are injured or incapacitated during your trip.

You can take steps to make sure that you are prepared when you arrive at your destination:

- Be well rested before you travel.
- Avoid long nighttime drives to rural or out-of-the-way locations.
- Dress casually and comfortably. Try not to stand out as a stranger.
- Go to your local destination promptly. Look carefully at the things you see along the way, making mental notes of what you may want to avoid.
- Avoid areas known for high crime rates or recent acts of terrorism.
- Travel with people you trust, even another traveler you have met on the way.
- Avoid budget hotels. They are often the site of drug and other illegal activity.
- Check out the hotels where you plan to stay before committing yourself to stay there.
- Take only those credit cards and other items you know you will need. Remove all unnecessary items from your wallet.
- If you wear glasses, take an extra pair with you.
- Leave a complete copy of your itinerary at your home and office.
- If a business trip, keep company phone numbers and your host's phone numbers, including home phone numbers, with you when you travel.
- Review your organization's travel policy.

7.3 AUTOMOBILES

Use common sense and extra precautions when you are driving on your trip, especially if you are driving in a foreign country. Specially trained drivers are usually available at high-risk destinations. Before you go, orient yourself to maps of airports, hotels, and public transportation routes. Carry or rent dependable communications devices. See Chapter 8: Automobiles for more detailed personal security information related to driving.

- Equip your vehicle with an alarm, hands-free communication system, GPS navigation, and radio (for public emergency and road condition reports).
- Ensure preventative maintenance before a long trip or lease a vehicle from a reputable agency.
- Always keep change with you for cab or bus fare or for telephone calls in case of an emergency.
- Always alarm, lock the car and take the keys.
- Always know your route when you leave on an unfamiliar trip. Be certain that you have enough money to get you there and back.
- Keep your wallet or purse and other valuables out of sight. Do not leave them on the seat next to you.
- Drive with all the doors locked and the windows rolled up. Use the driver's window if you need ventilation, since you can close it quickly if you need to.
- Do not pick up hitchhikers and never hitchhike yourself.
- If you see another motorist in trouble, do not stop. Signal to the motorist that you are getting help. Drive to the nearest phone in a safe place and call the police.
- If you are ever followed while driving, **do not drive to your hotel or pull over to the side of the road**. Go to the nearest police or fire station, stop in front, and keep honking your horn until someone comes out and you can report the incident. Or, drive to an open store or gas station where you can safely call the police.
- If someone bumps into your car, or if someone suspicious approaches you at a stop sign or intersection, honk your horn in short bursts.
- Do not hide a spare set of keys in a secret place − a thief will not be fooled by the place you select.

7.4 HOTEL SECURITY

Hotel rooms and elevators require special alertness to personal security issues. The first step is to select your hotel carefully.

- Select a hotel for its safety and security history. As a general rule, large international hotels, located in the better parts of town, are likely to be the most secure. If traveling on business, stay in company-designated hotels.

- Do not select a hotel on price alone. Consider the area in which the hotel is located. Drug dealers, intoxicated persons, and criminals are more apt to be found at budget hotels in high-crime areas.
- Watch for warning signs that a hotel has security problems. If you find any of the following, move on to another hotel:
  - An unusual amount of foot traffic through the parking lot could mean drug or gang activity.
  - A hotel without a resident security staff.
  - Liquor stores or all-night entertainment spots in the area can draw loiterers and vagrants.
  - A hotel with only outside entrances to the rooms. Outside entrances makes it too easy for an attacker to hide undetected.
- Look for hotels with proactive security, including the following:
  - Access control (card key), security staff, and CCTV surveillance
  - A well-lit and regularly patrolled parking lot.
  - Inside corridors for room entrances. Normally criminals will not enter well-lit interiors when there are other more opportune areas.
  - Visible patron and employee activity. Criminals are likely to avoid areas where they might be seen and discovered in the act.
- Stay in a room on floors three to five as a general rule. These floors are generally out of reach of criminals but within reach of fire ladders. Avoid ground-level rooms as a precaution.
- Ask a bellhop or someone you are traveling with to accompany you to your room to examine it before you unpack.
- Check your room for the following fire and security requirements:
  - Door locks and window locks in good working condition.
  - Windows inaccessible to other people using a balcony or fire escape.
  - A smoke detector, floor plan and fire exit map (usually on the back of your door), and a room safe.
- Know where your room key is at all times. Do not display your key carelessly or conspicuously in public places, such as the dining room or at the pool.
- Do not carry or display large amounts of cash or other valuables. Use the security provided by the hotel (for example, safes or safe deposit boxes). Carry a copy of your passport and let need-to-know officials know where the original is being kept.
- Use the hotel's main entrance when returning at night.

- Be suspicious of unusual calls or messages directed to your room.
- Do not let strangers enter your room without first getting positive identification. Call the front desk to verify that someone asked for your room.
- Double-lock your door when you are in your room, using the dead-bolt or chain. Consider carrying a portable lock. A wide body rubber doorstop can provide robust additional protection when securely placed under the door.
- When you leave your room for the day, do not tell the staff of your departure or when you plan to return. Do not turn in your key to the front desk. Leave a radio or television on and hang your "Do Not Disturb" sign.
- Do not leave proprietary information in your room when you leave for the day. Do not conduct sensitive discussions in your room or over the phone in your room.
- Ask for specific directions to your destination when you leave. Take the safest and most direct route.

7.4.1 Elevator Security
- Check the elevator before entering. If you feel uneasy about anyone in the elevator, wait for the next one.
- When you are waiting for the elevator to arrive, stand away from the door to avoid being pushed inside when the elevator arrives.
- When you enter the elevator, stand near the control panel. This will enable you to press the alarm button and as many of the other floor buttons as possible in case you have a problem.
- Wait until the other passengers press their floor buttons before you press the button for your floor.
- Stay alert. Look around at the other passengers. If anyone makes you uncomfortable, get off at the next floor. Do not continue to your room. Go to the lobby and request an escort.
- If you are accosted, push all the buttons on the control panel, including the **Alarm** button. Do not push the **Stop** button. Yell "Fire!" or "Help!" and try to get off at each floor.
- Often it is best not to ride with just one other person in an elevator if that person is a stranger. An elevator that has a moderate number of people is the safest.
- Report any elevator malfunction to the hotel staff immediately.

7.5 AIRPORTS

Airports and airlines are still favorite targets of terrorists and criminals. Most airports have responded to these activities by installing sophisticated detection equipment and inspection procedures. The best personal security measures, however, involve using common sense and planning carefully.

- When you select airlines and airports, pay close attention to their safety and security history. If traveling on business, your employer can help you identify the airlines and airports that have good records.
- Plan your trip around known weather conditions and similar delays.
- Whenever possible, avoid circuitous routes that involve long layovers. Try to travel nonstop from point of departure to point of destination.
- Arrive at the airport well in advance of departure for international flights due to the time required for preboarding screening, check-ins, and immigration checks.
- Do not over-pack your luggage. Even the sturdiest luggage can open under the rigors of baggage handling.
- Be certain that all your luggage has proper identification on the outside. Use your business address, not your home address. Place identification inside in a conspicuous place. Secure your luggage with a strap or tie, or place a seal across the zipper.
- Do not store valuables or prescriptions in your luggage. Pack important and valuable items in your carry-on luggage.
- Keep close control of all your luggage, tickets, and other important documentation.
- Spend as little time as possible in public places. Once you have completed your check-in, proceed to the safe areas behind the security checkpoint.
- Do not accept packages or parcels from anyone. These items could contain contraband, which could cause you serious problems.
- Avoid using public transportation. Use airport- or hotel-designated taxis or limos. Do not accept a ride from a low-cost transportation service. Whenever practical, arrange ground transportation in advance. Know the names of the people who will be meeting you.
- Get specific directions to your destination before you leave the airport.

7.6 INTERNATIONAL TRAVEL

International travel can offer many business opportunities as well as possibilities for personal enrichment. Traveling overseas, however, requires special preparation. All-hazards risk awareness is key to a safe and secure trip. Check with the US Overseas Security Advisory Council or your country's equivalent travel office.

7.6.1 Planning for International Travel

Before you travel abroad:

- Leave a copy of your complete itinerary and passport with hotel and host contacts, at your home and office. Restrict the knowledge of your travel plans to those people who have a need to know.
- Choose airlines that have good safety records. Select direct flights, avoiding intermediate stops.
- Make inquiries for credit, debit, traveler's checks, or cash security practices at your destination with your bank or card provider.
- Make photocopies of your passport or visa and the credit cards you plan to take with you. Pack two additional recent passport photos.
- Remove all the credit cards or identification you will not be using from your wallet.
- Check in advance about any vaccination requirements for the countries you plan to visit. Pack any medicine you plan to take in its original containers. Talk to your pharmacist about the generic names for the medication to facilitate refills. Check with your doctor to ensure that your medication does not violate foreign laws.
- Make sure all passport and visa requirements are satisfied.
- Obtain a country risk assessment and security briefing from the US Overseas Advisory Council or your home country embassy or diplomatic service. Let your embassy know your itinerary in advance so they may advise you of evolving risks.
- Have all the names, addresses, and phone numbers of your hotels in hand before you go.
- Do not make hotel reservations without the advice of your hosts.
- Consider purchasing extra luggage insurance. Claim settlements on international flights are known for being less than the value of the luggage.
- Place your tickets in a safe place on your person or in carry-on luggage. Treat your tickets like money, since they are readily convertible to cash.

- Make sure to send messages to trusted associates or loved ones at the beginning and completion of travel legs.

7.6.2 When You Reach Your Location

When you reach your destination outside of the United States, it will be prudent to increase your personal awareness of your surroundings. Some countries have higher risks due to higher crime rates associated with economically depressed areas; to actions from governments hostile to US policies; and to terrorism, criminal extortion, and threat.

- Contact the US Embassy to inform them of your presence in the country. Request any updates for country risk information.
- It is prudent to heed all the warnings and advice provided by your host, employer, your trusted hotelier, and government.
- Coordinate all your movements with your host. Use recommended transportation. Verify that a taxi or limo is the one you ordered before getting in. Avoid traveling alone. Avoid public transportation.
- Always avoid traveling in remote places and stay away from locations that have a history of trouble.
- Know how to use the public telephones. Carry the necessary coins to make emergency calls. Rent or buy devices from reputable service providers or add international calling to your domestic phone plan.
- Learn key phrases of the local language. Know how to contact your embassy and local authorities.
- Patronize only reputable hotels and restaurants.
- Once you are in a hotel, familiarize yourself with exits, door locks, window locks, and escape paths. Consider using a portable lock on your door.

For more information, see the *Airports* and *Hotel* Security sections earlier in this chapter.

7.7 VISITING THE UNITED STATES

All-hazards risk mitigation preparedness is no different when visiting the United States. Like any other country, there are differences in the level of personal risk from location to location, and from situation to situation. Taking sensible precautions can reduce your risk and help you stay safe during your visit in the United States.

Some types of man-made (crime) and natural risks are more prevalent in the United States than in other countries. It is important that you follow the personal security procedures associated with the particular types of crime most likely to occur in the United States.

If you are planning to relocate to the United States for work, your organization should provide you with additional materials to help you make a safe transition to your new home and job. You may also want to read the following chapters in this book:

- Chapter 2: Personal Protection
- Chapter 3: Assault and Sexual Assault
- Chapter 4: Children
- Chapter 5: Home Safety and Security
- Chapter 8: Automobiles
- Chapter 13: Fraud

7.8 PREPARING TO LIVE OUTSIDE THE UNITED STATES

No agency, application, hardware, person, solution, or technique can be relied upon to provide you with total safety. You and your family's well-being while abroad is a responsibility that **you** and **your family members** must undertake.

Even though high-risk conditions seem to be on the rise throughout the world, convincing people to introduce effective safety and security measures into their lives continues to be a difficult task. It is easy for people to feel that they will not be victims of all-hazards risk. However, by not being personally involved in the task of protecting yourself, your loved ones, and your property, you greatly increase your vulnerability.

Diverse climates, conditions, customs, and a wide range of other variables make it impossible to apply standard safety and security precautions world-wide. The precautions you implement should be consistent with the level of risk you face in the country to which you are moving.

You may need to adapt to cultural norms, customs, and laws that are very different from the ones you are accustomed to. Establishing a family residence abroad requires much more attention to risk than a short visit for business or pleasure.

CHAPTER 8

Automobiles

8.1 OVERVIEW

Automobiles are an integral part of most people's lives: as they go to work, run errands, go on vacation, and accomplish day-to-day tasks. Because they are such an everyday necessity, taking precautionary steps to reduce your personal risk in and around your car is an important part of protecting yourself and others.

This chapter provides some tips on reducing your personal risk in four automobile-related areas:

1. Theft
2. When you are driving
3. Parking your car
4. Carjacking

8.2 THEFT

Your car does not have to be new or expensive to interest car thieves. Professional car thieves often strip a car and sell its parts. No car is theft-proof; however, you can decrease the likelihood that your car will be stolen or burglarized by following a few simple steps.

8.2.1 Locking Your Car
Always lock your car and take the keys with you. If you park your car in a lot where you must leave the keys, leave only the ignition key with

the attendant. Other keys can easily be duplicated while you are gone. Do not mark your key chain with any personal identifying information, such as your name or car license number.

- Leaving your keys in the ignition not only makes it easy for a thief to steal your car, it is against the law.
- Do not hide extra keys under the hood or on the frame. A determined thief will find them.
- Close and lock all the doors and windows, including the vent windows and tailgate (if applicable).
- A locking gas cap can both prevent the theft of gasoline and limit the distance a thief can drive your car if it is stolen.
- Locks are also available for other marketable parts of your car, such as the battery, wheels, and electronic equipment.

8.2.2 Hiding Valuables
Do not leave packages, clothing, purses, or other valuable items in plain view inside your car. This includes electronic items such as cell phones, computers, or tablets. Valuables invite curiosity. If possible, take your valuables with you. Otherwise, store them in the trunk. Do not move items to your trunk at the spot where you are parking your car; a would-be thief may be watching.

8.2.3 Preventing Towing
To prevent thieves from towing your car, park it so that the drive wheels are close to a building, another vehicle, or an obstruction. For example, if your vehicle has front wheel drive, pull into a parking space. If your vehicle has rear wheel drive, back into the space. Always turn the steering wheel all the way to the right or the left before you shut off the ignition.

8.2.4 Anti-Theft Devices and Burglar Alarms
Anti-theft devices, such as steering column locks and burglar alarms, do deter thieves. They may not stop a professional thief, but they often scare off an amateur or a joyrider.

Auto theft investigators suggest that one of the best anti-theft devices, if used properly, is a mechanical device that locks to the steering wheel, column, or brake to prevent the steering wheel from being turned more than a few degrees. Commonly called j-bars, clubs, or collars, these devices must be installed correctly to be effective.

Remember, spending money on anti-theft devices will not help if you do not practice the basics: locking your car, taking the keys, and using your anti-theft devices.

8.2.5 Working with Law Enforcement Agencies

There are several things you can do to help law enforcement agencies recover stolen cars and catch car thieves.

- Look for your vehicle identification number (or serial number), write it down, and store it somewhere outside of the vehicle. A stolen car can often be recovered if its identification number is known.
- You may want to join Operation Identification (discussed in Chapter 5: Home Safety and Security) and have your car's serial number engraved in some hidden place on the car. This helps to identify your car even if the original serial number has been removed.
- Drop your business card or a piece of paper with your name and address on it into the window channel of your car door.
- If you buy a used car, look for signs that the proof of ownership may have been falsified. Ask questions such as where the current owner bought the car and where it is being serviced. Check the car for signs of forced entry or tampering. Examine the title and other documents for signs of forgery or alteration.
- Vehicle-related thefts happen at all hours of the day and night. If you see or hear something suspicious, such as someone looking into or ducking around cars, the popping sound of breaking glass, or someone tampering with a car, get a description of the suspects, notify authorities, and stay on the line. By reporting suspicious activity you could save yourself or your neighbor from being victimized.

8.3 WHEN YOU ARE DRIVING

As you drive, protect yourself by practicing the following safety precautions:

- Checking in and around your car before you get in and out, and keeping your doors locked and windows rolled up.
- Keeping your car in good repair, with your gas tank at least one quarter full.
- Traveling a safe distance from other cars and from pedestrians.

- Staying alert for vehicles that may be following you.
- Offering the right kind of assistance to people who may need help.
- Knowing what to do if your car breaks down.
- Planning ahead: Know the locations of police stations, fire departments, and busy shopping centers on your route.
- Using hands-free communications and GPS devices.

8.3.1 Check in and Around Your Car before Getting In and Out

Have your keys ready before you approach your car. As you approach, check underneath it and around it. Before you get in, check the trunk to ensure it's locked and check the front and back seats to be certain the car is empty. As you drive, keep the doors locked and the windows rolled up all the way.

When you arrive at your destination, do not unlock the car door until you have unfastened your seat belt, gathered your things, and looked around the area. If you must travel after dark, try to travel with a group or with an escort. If possible, install an automatic garage door opener that will open the door, turn on the light, and close the door before you get out of your car.

8.3.2 Keep Your Car in Good Repair and Your Tank One-Quarter Full

Use a reliable service station to keep your car in good repair. Do not travel long distances or in unknown areas if your car has a history of mechanical issues. Keep your tank at least one-quarter filled at all times.

Always keep sufficient spare change in your car to use a public telephone, or to take public transportation or call a cab, in case your car does break down.

8.3.3 Travel a Safe Distance from Other Cars and Pedestrians

Keep a reasonable distance from the car in front of you when you are driving. This will allow you to maneuver away from a threatening situation. On crowded streets, drive in the left or middle lane, away from the sidewalk, thereby making it more difficult for a pedestrian to reach inside your car. Keep your valuables out of sight.

If you drive a car with a manual transmission, stay in a driving gear when you are stopped at intersections, at stop signs, or for other reasons. You may need to react quickly if someone tries to get into your car.

8.3.4 Stay Alert for Vehicles that May Be Following You

If you think you are being followed, go to the nearest public place—a police station, a fire station, a hospital emergency entrance, or an all-night business establishment—and call for help immediately.

If you know you are being followed, attract attention by honking your horn and blinking your lights. As long as your car is operable, stay in it and keep the motor running. Do not pull over if someone signals to you by pointing at your tires, honking a horn, or otherwise indicating that something is wrong with your car. This is a common ploy to get you to stop your car.

If you think something may actually be wrong with your car, drive to a service station or public place where it is safer to stop. Keep an eye on the other driver to be certain that you are not being followed.

8.3.5 Offer the Right Kind of Assistance to People Who May Need Help

Do not stop to help a motorist in trouble. Signal to the other driver that you will get help. Then drive to the nearest phone and call the police for assistance. Never pick up a hitchhiker, whether male or female.

8.3.6 Know What to Do if Your Car Breaks Down

You are most vulnerable when your car breaks down (or runs out of gas) in an unfamiliar area.

- Always keep sufficient spare change in your car to use a public telephone, or to take public transportation or call a cab, in case your car does break down.
- Always keep your phone charged.
- If someone stops to assist you, do not let that person get into your car. Ask that person to call the police or a repair truck for you. Do not get out of your car until identified help arrives.

8.3.7 Plan Ahead

It's good to know the locations of police stations, fire departments, hospitals, and busy shopping centers on your route. If you are being followed, or if you need to call for assistance for someone else, knowing these locations can save valuable time.

Before you leave, tell someone you trust where you are going and when you expect to return. Travel on main roads when possible. Know where well-lit, attended parking lots are in relation to your destination.

8.4 PARKING YOUR CAR

Parked cars provide opportunities for theft, both of the car and of the items in the car; they also present security risks for the driver and other passengers as they leave and enter the car.

When you park your car — whether at work, when you go out for errands or entertainment, when you travel, or at home — you can decrease the opportunities for theft and reduce your personal risk by taking a few precautions. The same principles of parking lot safety discussed in Chapter 2: Personal Protection and Chapter 6: Workplace Safety and Security apply when parking your car anywhere.

8.5 CARJACKING

Carjacking is stealing a car by force. Carjacking has been on the increase and is getting more attention from the media. However, your chances of being a carjacking victim are very small. In this section, you will find information about basic carjacking facts and preventative actions.

8.5.1 Basic Carjacking Facts: Who, What, and Where

Many local and state criminal codes do not define carjacking as a separate crime. It is usually reported as either auto theft or armed robbery. Unfortunately, this means that there are not yet solid statistics on the times, places, and characteristics of the criminals and the victims.

We do know, however, that some places and times offer a higher degree of risk than others. The riskiest situations include:

- large parking lots close to major highways;
- stop lights and stop signs;
- parking garages that are unattended, dark, or relatively isolated;
- freeway ramps, where cars slow down or stop before merging with traffic;
- gas stations, especially self-serve gas stations;

- self-serve car washes;
- automated teller machines (ATMs);
- garages and parking lots that are connected to shopping malls or grocery stores, or that serve as mass transit park-and-ride locations;
- residential driveways and on residential streets as people get into and out of cars; and
- late at night. Though carjackings can occur at any time, a sizable share appear to take place during the late night hours.

Carjacking is not just a problem in large cities. It also happens in suburbs, small towns, and rural areas. Carjackers look for any opportunity. They do not choose victims by sex, race, or age. Often a carjacker bumps another car from the rear. As the driver gets out to check the damage and exchange information, one of the carjackers jumps into the victim's car and drives off.

8.5.2 Preventative Actions

By taking a few precautions, you can reduce your risk of being involved in a carjacking.

- Whenever you approach your car, walk with purpose and stay alert. Have your keys in hand. Look around, under, and in the car before getting in.
- On the road, keep your doors locked and windows rolled up. At stop signs, leave enough room between your car and other cars that you can drive away from a developing situation. Drive in the center lane to make it difficult to approach your car.
- Avoid driving alone, particularly at night, if possible. If you see someone stranded on the road, drive to the nearest telephone to call for help. Do not stop to assist strangers.
- If you are bumped by another car, look around before you get out. Make sure there are other cars around. Observe the car that rear-ended you and the people in it.
- If the situation makes you uneasy, jot down the car's license number and description, and signal the other car to follow you. Drive to the nearest police station or to a busy, well-lighted area. Call the police and wait for them to arrive if you have a cell phone with you.
- If you do get out of the car, take your keys, purse or wallet, and cell phone, if you have one. Stay alert.

- If you become involved in a potential carjacking situation, remember that your life is much more important than your car. Give up the car if threatened with a gun or weapon. Get away from the area as quickly as possible.
- Note the sex, race, age, hair and eye color, and any special features of the carjacker. Report the crime to the police immediately.
- When you park your car, remember to park in well-lit areas and keep all valuables locked up and out of sight. Always be aware of your surroundings.

8.6 OTHER HAZARD MITIGATION

Ensure your ability to safely communicate any high-risk condition to public safety.

- Equip your vehicle with hands-free communications and GPS, and use smartphone apps that communicate your location safely and instantaneously.
- Carry any necessary automobile device charger.
- Be prepared for severe weather or natural disaster with supplies including non-perishable food and water, rain or snow gear, jumper cables or battery recharger, flashlight, road flares, and emergency first aid kit.
- Consult your automobile club or public safety resources for additional risk mitigation tips.

CHAPTER 9

Locks and Alarms

9.1 OVERVIEW

Being secure in your home is one of the most important parts of personal security. Most of the information on the procedures to follow in your home is covered in Chapter 5: Home Safety and Security. This chapter and Chapter 10: Lighting provide information on the physical and equipment aspects of security.

This chapter covers door locks, window locks, alarm systems, selecting an alarm company, and building codes.

9.2 DOOR LOCKS

Locking the doors and windows in your home is the most effective way to increase home security. Proper selection, installation, and use of locks are the keys to securing doors and windows.

- Use locks that allow you to get out of the house quickly in case of an emergency.
- Be certain to lock all the doors and windows—it only takes one unsecured opening to allow an intruder easy entry.
- Every door in your home that leads to the outside should have two locks:
  1. A standard door latch (usually the kind that is included with door handle kits). These locks are also called cylindrical or key-in-knob locks. From a security standpoint, these locks are the least desirable.
  2. A dead bolt, slide bolt, or chain.

- Ensure that the latch plates are secured to the door frame with at least three-inch wood screws.

9.2.1 Dead Bolt Locks

Dead bolt locks are the best way to secure doors that lead to the outside.

- Be certain that the dead bolt has at least a one-inch throw (i.e., the bolt extends at least one inch past the door frame when the door is in a locked position).
- For doors that do not have a dead bolt, add one that has the same key as the knob. You can easily find stores that will create a key for a dead bolt that matches an existing key.
- Dead bolts that use keys on both sides should be used when the inside lock and knob is accessible through an adjoining window pane or when the door has glass as part of its construction.
- Where solid wood or steel doors without side window panes are installed, a thumb latch may be used to secure the inside of the door.
- Do not leave keys in keyways. Place a key by the door for emergency use.

9.2.2 Slide Bolt Locks

Slide bolt locks install on the inside of the room.

- Slide bolts are useful for securing doors from the inside in rooms where you enter through a different door (such as a basement door).
- As with dead bolts, be certain that the bolt extends at least one inch beyond the door when it is in a locked position.

9.2.3 Chain Locks

Chain locks are used in the same situations as slide bolts. Be certain that the chain is sturdy and installed properly.

9.2.4 Other Ways to Secure Doors

- Install a viewing device to see who's at the door before opening it. Use a swing bar or chain to allow the door to open only a few inches.
- Pin the door hinges. This involves drilling a small hole through the hinge and through the hinge pin and then putting a nail in the hole.
- Be certain all exterior doors are made of solid wood or solid-core metal.

- Double doors, like French doors, should have sliding bolts at the top and the bottom. Use a piece of wood or broomstick to keep sliding glass doors and patio doors from opening even if the lock is defeated.

9.3 WINDOW LOCKS

Like doors, windows are the most likely entrance to your home for an intruder.

- Standard clamshell or butterfly locks are not good deterrents. They serve mostly to hold the window sashes together to reduce drafts and rattling.
- The most effective locks are those with keys. Key locks can be either the turnbuckle or the bolt variety.
- If a window is used for ventilation, install locks that allow the window to be locked in an open position. For example, if you are using key bolt locks, install two sets on each window. Install one at the locked level and one at the open level (three to four inches above the locked level).

9.3.1 Other Ways to Secure Windows

Other ways to further secure your windows include:

- Replace single-pane glass with double-glaze glass. Use wire-embedded glass for increased protection against breakage.
- Install shutters or grates.
- Pin the window. Close the window tightly and drill a small hole through the top sash of the bottom part of the window and partway through the bottom sash of the top part. Then insert a small pin that is easy to remove from the inside when you want to open the window.

9.4 ALARM SYSTEMS AND SECURITY SURVEILLANCE

An alarm system and cameras can increase the security of your home when properly installed and used. Some of the advantages of owning an alarm system include the following:

- Discouraging intruders before they try to force an entry.
- Increasing the value of your property.

- Rate reductions on property insurance.
- Reporting dangerous conditions including accidents, duress, fire, or intrusion.
- Documenting criminal conduct or other unsafe conditions.
- Summoning emergency assistance.

But, there are also disadvantages:

- False alarms caused by system failures or improper use, and the associated municipal fines.
- A false sense of security that leads people to dismiss the fundamentals of home security—most commonly, not locking doors and windows.

If you are considering an alarm system, be certain that it is of high quality. Purchase the system from a reputable company. Be certain that you and the other members of your family know how to use the system. On a regular basis, check to see that procedures are being followed and that the system is still working.

9.4.1 Power Supplies

Alarm and camera systems are only as good as their power supplies and communication network connectivity. The most dependable system operates on household power with emergency battery power. Systems can also be powered by batteries alone. In this case, be certain that the system includes a way to automatically report battery failure. In addition, try to obtain a service and maintenance contract that includes automatic battery replacement when needed.

9.4.2 Warranties

Be certain that the company you deal with provides a warranty and prompt service whenever a malfunction occurs on your alarm system. The warranty should cover all parts and labor, for both the manufacturer and the installer.

Malfunctions are always possible whenever electrical equipment is being used. A good system gives a visual and/or audible signal whenever the system malfunctions (for example, in the event of a power failure or a component failure).

9.4.3 Local Crime Prevention Programs

It is very important that you work with your local crime prevention programs. Your alarm and/or camera system should be part of the crime prevention efforts in your community.

• Register your system properly.
• Advise local law enforcement agencies who to contact if you are not available when your system gives an alarm signal.
• Cooperate with your local police department's requirements and requests.

9.4.4 Alarm System Components

Alarm systems have three basic components: a master control panel, a control pad, and sensors. Local code may require specific panels or reporting capabilities for burglary, duress, fire, or other life safety or property risk conditions (carbon monoxide, radon, etc.).

The master control panel is sometimes called the communications board. It is the "brains" of the system — it is connected to the sensors and often to the telephone line to place calls automatically to police and fire departments. The master control panel interprets signals sent from the sensors, accepts instructions from users, and triggers alarms.

The control pad is usually a numeric key pad that is used to enter codes and other instructions. Often, the control pad is connected to the master control panel.

Sensors can be any of a large variety of devices that detect motion, heat, weight, sound, or an interrupted signal. Some of the most common types of sensors used in home security systems are listed and expanded upon below.

• Contacts (magnetic and plunger)
• Glass break detectors
• Motion detectors
• Pressure mats
• Duress alarms
• Gas, Smoke, and Rate-of-Rise Heat Detectors

9.4.4.1 Contacts (Magnetic and Plunger)

The most widely used alarm sensors are contacts. These are electro-mechanical devices comprised of a simple switching mechanism or concealed contact buttons. Contacts are attached to doors, windows, and other entry points. When the entry point is opened, the magnet moves away from the switch or the plunger (similar to the hidden light switch on automobile and refrigerator doors) and the alarm sounds.

9.4.4.2 Glass Break Detectors

These are special sensors that react to sound and other vibrations. They are often sensitive to the sound of broken glass, but they can also be used to detect vibrations in walls and doors. Problem-free operation of these kinds of detectors depends on close attention to the design of the system and the sensitivity levels of the detectors.

9.4.4.3 Motion Detectors

These devices transmit a radio frequency and are programmed to respond to any change that occurs in the return frequency. Motion within range of these detectors' signal pattern alters the return frequency and triggers an alarm.

9.4.4.4 Pressure Mats

Generally used under rugs or carpets, these mats are really flat switches that react to pressure from footsteps. They are often placed in doorways, hallways, window areas, and staircases, where they can be used to isolate specific areas.

Since large pets and small children can cause a fair number of false alarms with this type of sensor, be certain that pressure mats can be turned off independently of other alarm system sensors.

9.4.4.5 Duress Alarms

These devices are small buttons that may be located at various spots within the home, particularly alongside entrance doors and next to beds. You only need to push the button to activate the alarm system. Duress alarms are useful if you suspect an intruder is in your home or if someone tries to force entry when you answer the door. Proper location, installation, and training are required to ensure that panic buttons are not pushed by children, other curious people, or by pets.

9.4.4.6 Gas, Smoke, and Rate-of-Rise Heat Detectors

These fire and life-safety devices are often dictated by local fire code with special panel and communications requirements. Check with reputable safety and security solution providers and public safety agencies for recommendations and requirements.

9.5 SELECTING AN ALARM COMPANY

The alarm systems industry is one of the country's fastest growing. While there are many experienced and reliable companies, there are also those who are out to take advantage of the concerned homeowner.

When you look for an alarm systems company, check out several companies, select a well-established company with a good record, and be certain that you understand how the system works before you buy.

9.5.1 Check Out Several Companies

Contact at least three reputable alarm systems companies before you make a purchase. Look online on customer review sites and check with your friends to find the names of companies with whom you may want to do business.

Make an appointment with each company representative to appraise your security needs and discuss cost factors. Obtain a written proposal from each company. Do not sign the proposal until you are ready to select the company to install your system.

9.5.2 Select a Well-Established Company with a Good Record

It is important that the company you select has a history of successful operation. Before you purchase, talk to some of the current customers of the companies you are considering.

- Reputable companies will not hesitate to provide you with names of satisfied customers.
- Ask the customers about the system's performance and the service they have received from the company.
- Check with people in your community who have security systems. Find out about their experiences.

9.5.3 Understand How the System Works before You Buy

- Be certain that you receive written instructions on how to use the system and that you have practiced using the system.
- Know how the system uses your telephone lines to place calls when the alarm is activated.
- Find out about maintenance, service, and warranties before you commit to a purchase.

9.6 BUILDING CODES

Many cities have crime prevention building codes for homes, stores, restaurants, apartment complexes, and hotels. If you are doing any building or remodeling, check with your city's building inspector's office for information on any building codes that may apply.

Lighting

10.1 OVERVIEW

Lighting and security go hand in hand. Statistics show that increases in lighting levels around homes and businesses have been responsible for decreases in the amount of criminal activity. Lights, when properly installed, used, and kept in good working condition, can deter burglary, vandalism, assault, and many other types of crime.

This chapter covers three basic lighting issues:

1. General guidelines
2. Residential lighting
3. Security lighting

10.2 GENERAL GUIDELINES

Effective use of lighting in and around your home and community can help prevent or mitigate accidents, crimes, injuries, property damages, or other liabilities. To be effective, consider these lighting guidelines:

- Use efficient light sources.
- Use lights and reflective paint to improve parking lot visibility.
- Carefully place security floodlights.
- Use materials that reflect light.
- Apply perimeter lighting when possible.
- Control lights with timers and motion detectors for energy conservation.

10.2.1 Use Efficient Light Sources

Light sources that have been proven to produce maximum light output for lower cost and energy use include

- high-pressure sodium lamps;
- metal halide lamps;
- deluxe white high-intensity discharge lamps; and
- solar powered light-emitting diode (LED) walkway illuminator.

10.2.2 Use Lights and Reflective Paint to Improve Parking Lot Visibility

In parking lots at night, it is important that people are able to clearly see other people as they approach their car. Good lighting also enables people to quickly locate and identify their car. By illuminating parking lots with efficient light sources and by painting 24″ white or yellow stripes between parking spaces, you can help reduce incidents in your community's parking lots.

10.2.3 Carefully Place Security Floodlights

Security floodlighting should not be directed too far out from a building, nor should it be too high above the ground. When properly placed, security floodlights do not produce extremely light and dark areas or distracting glare. If you are placing security floodlights in an area, whether for your home, a business, or a community building, seek professional help for installation and placement.

10.2.4 Use Materials that Reflect Light

Use white paint or other light colors to reflect light and help illuminate dark areas, such as walkways, aisles, entrances, and exits. You can also use other highly reflective materials in these areas. If you need assistance finding these materials, talk to your public utilities company, local law enforcement agency, or crime prevention group.

10.2.5 Apply Perimeter Lighting When Possible

Perimeter lighting can serve as a light barrier deterrent to would-be intruders. Perimeter floodlights should be at least 75 feet away from the building. They should be installed around the entire building to illuminate all ground-floor openings in the building. If you need assistance in planning perimeter lighting, talk to your public utilities company, local law enforcement agency, or crime prevention group.

10.2.6 Motion Detectors and Timers

Motion detection lighting indoors and out enables residents to have just-in-time, hands-free lighting with considerable energy savings. Trespassers are more easily detected, deterred, and/or documented with integrated cameras while legitimate owners, renters, guests, and emergency responders have well-lit walkways as needed.

10.3 RESIDENTIAL LIGHTING

Lighting is generally divided into four types: indoor, safety, outdoor, and security.

These distinctions are somewhat arbitrary, since all well-used lighting adds to the security of the home. The distinctions focus on where the lights are placed and the kinds of lights used. The first three types are discussed in this section; security lighting is covered in the next section.

To provide protective lighting in and around your home, you should adhere to the following guidelines:

• Create a barrier of light all the way around your home.
• Work with your neighbors to create adequate lighting between homes.
• Use a proactive maintenance approach to be certain that all lights are working properly.
• Eliminate dark areas that can conceal criminals by lighting areas around alleys, trash bins, and storage sheds.
• Provide light around all gates and exterior entrances.
• Close your drapes at night.
• Use motion-detecting and timer-controlled lights.
• Leave a few lights on when you retire for the evening.

10.3.1 Indoor Lighting

Indoor lighting enhances security by providing the appearance that someone is home. Intruders are less likely to attempt to enter a home if it is occupied.

• Use timers to turn lights on and off when you are away.
• If your home is empty during the day, use a timer to turn on lights before the first person arrives home from work.

- Use a timer to leave a few lights on for a while when you retire for the evening. Occasionally, change to a different pattern of lights left on.

10.3.2 Safety Lighting

Safety lighting is the kind used to light entrances, steps, stairways, garages, and other places where it may be difficult to see at night.

- Safety lights should be turned on before dark so that people do not arrive in the dark.
- Light-sensitive devices can be used to turn on safety lights as it gets dark.
- Safety lights may need more maintenance than indoor lighting, since some safety lights are exposed to the elements.

10.3.3 Outdoor Lighting

Outdoor lighting is the kind used to light sidewalks, walkways, yards, and alleys. It does not have to be high voltage to be effective. However, it must shine its light on the target area. Be certain that the light fixture does not block the light from its intended target.

- Street lights often provide the only outdoor lighting for most homes.
- Use sufficient outdoor lighting to be able to identify a person.
- Use a timer, motion unit, or light-sensitive device to turn outdoor lights on and off.

10.4 SECURITY LIGHTING

While all lighting that is used properly in and around the home adds to the home's security, security lighting consists of those special lights designed to detect motion, heat, light, or sound, or to work as a part of an alarm system; and to illuminate areas that have a higher security risk.

10.4.1 Security Lights with Sensors

Security lights are often equipped with a sensor that detects motion, heat, light, or sound. In addition, lights may be connected to an alarm system. Whenever an alarm is activated, the lights are automatically turned on.

- Many home owners use a motion or heat detector to turn on security lights. Whenever someone passes through the detector's field, the light turns on. After a predetermined amount of time (for example, three minutes), if there has been no further motion or heat in the field, the light turns off.
- Use security lights with light-sensitive detectors in areas that have a high traffic volume. These lights turn on at dusk and stay on until morning.
- Use security lights with heat, motion, or sound detectors in areas that have a low traffic volume. They will turn on only when they are needed during night time hours.
- Many safety lights, especially the ones used to illuminate front and back door areas, can be converted to security lights.

10.4.2 Lighting High-Risk Areas

Security lighting for high-risk areas, such as alleys, outbuildings, parking areas, and other dark areas, usually must be installed by a professional.

- Use a timer or a light-sensitive device to turn lights on when it begins to get dark and off as the sun rises.
- Be certain that the electrical cable used to power these lights is positioned so that it is not easily accessible or likely to be damaged accidentally.
- Use energy-efficient lights that provide sufficient illumination. Be certain that they are correctly placed and directed.
- For large areas, such as yards or fenced-in areas, use floodlights or spotlights.

10.4.3 Security Lighting for Other Buildings

Although many offices, commercial buildings, schools, churches, and other community buildings use surveillance and guard services to provide security, lighting can be an effective addition to their security picture. For those buildings that do not have security guards, it is especially important to use lighting to increase security during nonbusiness hours.

- High-efficiency light sources should be used at all entrance and exit areas. From a security point of view, the entrance and exit areas are particularly critical.

- Security floodlights placed around the building can increase property protection as long as the glare of floodlights is minimized and the lights are directed at the building.
- Lighting fixtures need to illuminate as much of the building as possible, especially windows, doors, and other openings.
- Fenced-in areas should be lit from the fence line to the building.

CHAPTER 11

Drug and Alcohol Abuse

11.1 OVERVIEW

Drug and alcohol abuse have many serious consequences. They are major contributors to violence, both domestic and in public. Hundreds of innocent people are killed each year by drivers under the influence. The physical, intellectual, and emotional health of many adults and children are irreparably damaged by drug and alcohol abuse. The economy and taxpayers lose millions of dollars each year in medical treatment and lost worker productivity.

Preventing drug and alcohol abuse is an issue for personal security because it is closely related to individual health and safety. This chapter addresses four main areas of drug and alcohol abuse:

1. Education and awareness
2. In the workplace
3. Children and other family members
4. Community action

11.2 EDUCATION AND AWARENESS

Drug and alcohol abuse are not small problems that take care of themselves. People who become trapped by drugs or alcohol need help from friends, family, and associates.

- Learn to recognize the signs of drug and alcohol abuse.
- Talk to friends, relatives, or colleagues who show signs of drug or alcohol abuse.
- If you are an abuser, take control of your life.

11.2.1 Recognizing Signs of Drug and Alcohol Abuse

Recognizing the signs is an important first step in helping someone with a drug or alcohol abuse problem.

- Do the person's moods or activity level change quickly? Drugs can cause a person to become more irritable, secretive, withdrawn, angry, or very happy without any apparent cause.
- Has the person become less responsible? Does he or she have difficulty remembering things? For example, you might notice your child coming home late from school or other events, failing to do chores or homework, or becoming dishonest.
- Is the person changing friends or changing lifestyles? For instance, you might notice that your friend has new interests, has unexplained amounts of cash, or starts to dress and act very differently.
- Is the person difficult to communicate with? Does he or she avoid talking to you face to face and find it uncomfortable to be around the family?
- Is the person showing a sudden interest in drugs by talking or reading about them? Does he or she own paraphernalia?
- Does the person show physical deterioration? Show a marked loss of interest in appearance? Is he or she gaining or losing weight rapidly or having difficulty concentrating?
- Does the person have large amounts of cash? Is he or she chronically short of cash?
- Does the person have slurred or incoherent speech? Is he or she losing physical coordination, or beginning to take unusual risks?

11.2.2 Talk to Friends Who Show Signs of Drug or Alcohol Abuse

If you think someone you know is abusing drugs or alcohol, compare recent behavior with past behavior. It is better to say something and be mistaken than to ignore the issue and find out that you could have lent a helping hand.

- Plan ahead. Think about what you are going to say, and how you want to say it.
- Pick a quiet, private place to have the conversation. Do not talk to the person when he or she is high or drunk.
- Try to stay calm. Do not get into an argument.

- Let the person know that you care. Do not expect the person to like what you are saying, but stick with it.
- Get others to reinforce your message. The more people that get involved, the more likely the person will seek help.
- Look for help. Talk to someone who knows about drug and alcohol abuse and who can give you advice.
- Offer to help. Find out about local hot lines and other counseling possibilities. Offer to go with the person to seek professional help.

11.2.3 Take Control of Your Life

Remember that there are legal and ethical consequences for things you do under the influence of drugs and alcohol. Stay away from friends who need to use drugs or alcohol to have fun. Do not go to parties where you know you will be surrounded by people under the influence. Intravenous drug use places you at a high risk for contracting AIDS and other incurable diseases. If you are abusing drugs or alcohol, seek help. Talk to a close friend or seek professional help. See Chapter 14: Personal Security Resources for more information about contacting professional help. The sooner you recognize a problem, the sooner you are on the road to taking control of your life.

11.3 IN THE WORKPLACE

Most organizations make a firm commitment to maintaining a drug-free workplace. Often, an organization has an official policy on drug and alcohol use, and may offer support services through human resources. Everyone benefits from a drug-free workplace.

11.3.1 Some Facts About Employees Who Abuse Drugs and Alcohol

Employees who abuse drugs and alcohol have an immense negative effect on health, safety, and productivity.

- They work far less productively.
- They miss work more often.
- They are more likely to injure themselves or others compared to employees who do not abuse drugs.
- They file more workers' compensation claims.
- They add to the hidden costs of doing business through increased stress on the job, overtime to fill in for absent or tardy employees, demands

on the time of supervisors and coworkers, damage to company equipment, and the negative effect on the company's reputation.

Employers cannot absorb all the costs related to drug and alcohol abuse. Consequently, these costs are passed on to others, such as the company's employees (through higher insurance premiums) and consumers (through higher prices for products or services).

11.3.2 Signs that a Fellow Employee May Be Abusing Drugs or Alcohol

During the course of a working career, nearly everyone knows someone who used drugs or alcohol on the job. When you know that a coworker is using drugs or alcohol on the job, there are good reasons why you should get involved.

Below is a list of signs that may provide clues that a fellow employee is abusing drugs or alcohol.

- Frequent tardiness or absence
- Abrupt changes in mood or attitude
- Poor relationships with coworkers
- Poor concentration or uncharacteristic errors in judgment
- Deterioration of personal appearance and hygiene
- Decreases in job performance and productivity
- Frequent shortages of cash, with requests to borrow from coworkers or to receive advances on paychecks

11.4 CHILDREN AND OTHER FAMILY MEMBERS

Children are very susceptible to peer pressure and the urge to experiment, both of which make it difficult for parents to convince them not to try drugs and alcohol. The following checklist summarizes things you can do to help your children avoid drugs. For more information, see Chapter 4: Children.

11.4.1 Drug Checklist for Your Children

Don't put off talking to your children about drugs, and don't expect schools to do it all. Children need to see that their parents are involved.

- Start your children on a drug education program through your school or community group.

- Make sure children understand the difference between medications and street drugs.
- Use the common street names for street drugs when identifying them to your children.
- Explain the hazards and bad side-effects of using street drugs.
- Explain why some people use drugs and the problems they have.
- Use role-playing to teach children to say **No** to drugs.

11.4.2 Helping Your Spouse or Other Family Members

Many times, drug and alcohol abuse problems are just the symptoms of other problems in the family, including the following:

- Marital and relationship difficulties
- Legal and financial pressures
- Family conflicts and parenting issues
- Stress management
- Grief and loss

Recognizing the underlying problem is the first step in addressing drug and alcohol abuse. You may want to seek counseling or other help from professionals when a family member's problems seem to be more than you can handle on your own.

11.5 COMMUNITY ACTION

Communities across the nation have found effective ways to reduce drug and alcohol abuse by forming comprehensive partnerships. Effective partnerships can be made with the following groups:

- Law enforcement agencies
- Parents
- Schools
- Health professionals
- Community leaders
- Businesses
- Young people
- Tenant organizations
- Neighborhood leaders
- Religious organizations
- The media

Each partner has a key part to play as an educator, a strategist, someone who gets the word out, or as a participant performing a professional or community role. These partnerships are formed through networks that draw on diverse resources, using community-wide cooperation to meet common goals. Some of the actions your community can take are listed below:

- Ask police for assistance in forming a citizen patrol that walks the neighborhood, writing down license plate numbers and descriptions of known and suspected drug dealers, and photographing and videotaping drug-related activities.
- Use good judgment when faced with problems of illegal drug use or sales or other criminal activity in your neighborhood. Think about how you can report a drug problem without opening yourself up to the possibility of retaliation.
- Let restaurants, bars, landlords, and others who do business with or ignore drug dealers know that you are dissatisfied with their contributions to the drug problems. Use public demonstrations and hold vigils to show that your community has the will and commitment to driving out drugs.
- Organize community clean-up campaigns to remove drug paraphernalia and litter from the streets, paint over graffiti, plant flowers and trees, and repair broken items. Show people that your community cares about its appearance and that it is not helpless in the face of crime.
- Plan and develop a drug-free school zone with the cooperative efforts of law enforcement agencies, parents, youth organizations, and school officials. A drug-free school zone provides a solid framework on which to build a community-wide commitment to reducing drug use.
- Drug dealer properties are often run-down or abandoned buildings. Ask fire, health, and housing departments to inspect these buildings for code violations and to shut down these hazardous properties. Urge your city officials to tear down abandoned buildings or to sell them through civic programs for rehabilitation.
- Ask the police for more patrols. Perhaps a mini-station can be opened in your area.
- Establish a hot line where people can call to report suspicious activity anonymously to the police. Use volunteers to answer the phone.
- Use the law to make life difficult for drug dealers. Property owners can give police permission to enter private property such as parking

lots and outside stairs to investigate and arrest loiterers. Landlords can rewrite their leases to specifically ban drug activity. Businesses that sell drug paraphernalia can be closed down with zoning laws.

- Asset forfeiture laws, nuisance abatement laws, and drug-free zone laws can all be used to seize assets from convicted drug dealers, to bring suits against property owners who tolerate drugs and graffiti, and to increase the penalties for drug-related activities on school property.
- Contact your local district attorney's office for help and information about your area's laws.
- Find out who is responsible for towing abandoned cars in your area. Be persistent about reporting abandoned cars until they are removed.
- Telephone companies can fix pay phones so that only outgoing calls are possible. Public utilities can shut off service to buildings that are being used for illegal activities.
- Contact your local police department to organize a Neighborhood Watch program. Post large, colorful signs that give notice that people are watching and reporting drug-related activities and other crimes.
- Get young people involved in all of your community's anti-drug activities.

Seniors

12.1 OVERVIEW

Senior citizens have the right to live with dignity and to be as safe and secure as possible—personally, physically, and financially. Security for seniors involves the basic issues of

- understanding the fundamental ways to improve safety;
- increasing security at home;
- increasing security when walking, running errands, or going out for entertainment; and
- protecting money and financial security.

12.2 GENERAL TIPS TO INCREASE YOUR SAFETY

Older individuals are particularly vulnerable to con games, purse snatchers, and pickpockets. Even minor crimes can cause physical, emotional, and financial distress. Fear of crime can make a senior person feel helpless and lead to isolation. A general decrease in the quality of life is often the outcome of being afraid of becoming a crime victim. As a senior, you can take proactive steps to increase your safety and security and to remain in control of your life.

- Use common sense when you go out. Stay alert to your surroundings. Go out with friends or relatives.
- Do not carry large amounts of cash. Carry your purse in front of you, or carry your wallet in a front or inside pocket.

- Use direct deposit for any regularly repeating checks (for example, Social Security checks or pension checks).
- Install good locks on your windows and doors. Use the locks, even when you are only going out for a short time.
- Do not allow service or delivery people in without identification and an appointment. Call the company to verify that the person is a legitimate employee.
- Do not be taken in by investment schemes, security system schemes, sweepstakes, miracle cures, free check-ups or home inspections, or any other opportunity that sounds too good to be true. Things that sound too good to be true are always too risky for your involvement.
- Never sign anything with which you are not completely comfortable. Do not be rushed into any kind of an agreement. Take the information or contract to a person you trust.
- If you drive, lock your doors and roll up your windows. Never leave the keys in the car.
- If you ride public transportation, sit close to the driver or the exit.
- Get involved in your Neighborhood Watch program. Report any suspicious activity and any criminal activity.
- Volunteer to improve your community's well-being by working as a tutor, a block organizer, or as an office aide for the police department, the fire department, or a social service agency.

12.3 AT HOME

The best way to improve security at home is to make it difficult for intruders to get into your house. To increase your security at home, follow the guidelines below:

- Equip your doors with easy-to-obtain security features.
- Open and lock exterior doors carefully.
- Work with your neighbors to increase everyone's security.
- Know how to use your phone.
- Know what to do if you are awakened by an intruder.
- Do not keep large amounts of cash at home. Keep your money in a bank or a safe deposit box.

12.3.1 Equip Your Doors with Easy-to-Obtain Security Features

Equip your door with a dead bolt lock. Select a lock that has a cylinder that is protected by a guard plate. Install a viewer or peephole in each of the entrances. Select a viewer of the wide-angle type, which gives you a more complete view of the area outside your door. See Chapter 9: Locks and Alarms for more information.

12.3.2 Open and Lock Exterior Doors Carefully

Do not open an exterior door until you are sure of the identity of the visitor(s). Always lock the door when you leave, even if you are just going out to pick up the mail, walk a pet, or take out the trash.

If, upon your return, you find that the door is open or it looks like it has been tampered with, do not enter. Leave immediately and notify the police. If you lose your keys or if they are stolen, immediately replace your locks. Do not leave a key under the mat, in the mailbox, in an area near the door, or anywhere outside.

12.3.3 Work with Your Neighbors to Increase Everyone's Security

When you go away, even if it is only for one night, ask a neighbor you trust to pick up your mail and newspapers. Offer to do the same for them. If you are going away for a longer period of time, ask a trusted neighbor to check your place each day that you are gone. Have your mail held at your local post office so that deliveries do not accumulate.

12.3.4 Know How to Use Your Phone

When you answer the phone, do not volunteer information to any caller you do not know personally. If you have voicemail or an answering machine, do not provide your name or phone number on the outgoing message. If you don't have an answering machine, consider using one. An answering machine lets you monitor your incoming phone calls without answering the phone. Potential intruders often try to find out if someone is home before they attempt a break-in.

12.3.5 Know What to Do if You are Awakened by an Intruder

If you are awakened by an intruder, do not take any action unless you absolutely have to. Stay perfectly still, and try to stay calm. Call the police at the first **safe** opportunity.

12.4 WHEN YOU ARE WALKING, RUNNING ERRANDS, OR GOING OUT

The best defense against street crime is to stay alert and use common sense. Be aware of your surroundings, wherever you are. Trust your instincts. If you feel uncomfortable in a place or situation, leave quickly. When you go out, whether it is for a walk or other exercise, to run an errand, or for entertainment, following a few rules can improve your security dramatically.

12.4.1 If Possible, Do Not Go Out Alone

Use the buddy system whenever possible. There is safety in numbers. Travel and shop with companions whenever possible. Try to transact your business during daylight hours. When you go out in the evening, do not go out alone. Stay alert to the possibility that someone may attempt to follow you home.

12.4.2 Know How to Carry Your Purse, Your Wallet, and Other Valuables

Avoid carrying a purse or briefcase, if possible. It is easier for a thief to grab a larger object than to take a wallet. If you do need to carry a purse, use a shoulder strap and keep one hand under the purse. Keep your keys, cash, and credit cards in your pockets or somewhere else on your person. Avoid carrying large sums of money. If your purse, pocketbook, or wallet is snatched, let it go. If you fight for it, you may suffer a serious injury.

12.4.3 Carrying Weapons

If you carry a weapon, know how to use the available features. Be aware of the fact that weapons are often turned against the victim by the attacker. In addition, carrying a concealed weapon is illegal in most situations.

12.4.4 Walk and Drive Safely

Whether walking or driving, always use streets that are well-traveled and well-lit at night.

When you are walking, adhere to the following safety guidelines:

- Wait for a new green light or walk signal before starting to cross the street.

- Wait to cross a street until you can cross with other pedestrians.
- Be particularly alert for turning cars. Watch the driver's eyes before you cross in front of a turning car or a car that seems to be waiting for you.
- Check for traffic before stepping into a cross walk, even if you are crossing with the green light or walk signal.
- Be decisive when you cross a street. Do not stop in the middle to decide whether to turn back or go ahead.
- Never run across the street.
- Wear reflective clothing at night or carry a light to help drivers see you.
- Always cross at an intersection. If traffic is heavy, cross at a stop light, even if it means adding distance to your walk.

If you drive, follow these safety measures:

- Keep your car in good working order.
- Keep your gas tank filled at least one-quarter.
- Keep your doors locked and windows rolled up.
- Park in well-lit places.
- Always check the front and back seats before you get into the car.

See Chapter 8: Automobiles for more information on being secure when you are driving.

12.4.5 Know What to Do if You Are Ever Attacked

If you are being robbed, do not fight back. Give the thief what he or she wants. Try to focus on what the thief looks like, so that you can provide police with a description of height, weight, clothing, and any other identifying information. After an attack, notify the police as soon as you can and give them as much information as possible.

12.5 PROTECTING YOUR MONEY AND FINANCIAL SECURITY

Con artists prey on everyone, but senior citizens are especially vulnerable. Be suspicious of any proposal for home repairs, insurance, or investments that sound too good to be true. Never provide anyone with cash unless you have an enforceable guarantee. Be extremely cautious of any arrangement that has to be kept secret.

12.5.1 Protect Your Money

If a deal sounds too good to be true, it probably is. You should never give money, especially cash, to a stranger, and you only buy from legitimate, established companies. Most criminals attempt to sell unknown products or services by claiming to represent a company that you have never heard of.

Use a check, rather than a credit card or cash, when you make purchases. Although buying with a credit card is usually safe, criminals sometimes are successful at using your credit card number without your knowledge. If someone demands cash for a purchase, you can almost be assured that the seller is a criminal or engaged in illegal activities. If you are suspicious about a person trying to sell you something, do not make the purchase. Report the incident to the police.

12.5.2 Be Alert to Scams and Frauds

Thieves are more likely to target you if you receive regular checks, such as dividends, Social Security, pension, government assistance, or retirement payments. Some of the ways to avoid scams and frauds include the following:

- If possible, have your checks deposited electronically and automatically at your bank. This eliminates the regular arrival of checks in your mail.
- Use checks, not cash, when you make purchases.
- Use cashier's checks when you need to make large purchases.
- Do not give out your credit card numbers to unknown callers, or to anyone who offers a one-time-only deal.
- Investigate a company thoroughly before you do business with them.
- Watch out for phony sweepstakes, drawings, contests, prizes, and anything else that is aimed at getting your money before you can thoroughly check out the company.
- Call the Better Business Bureau, or even the police, before doing business with companies that make exaggerated or too-good-to-be-true offers.

12.5.3 Anti-Fraud Tips

- Do not give your credit card numbers or checking account information over the telephone unless you know exactly with whom you are dealing.
- Be skeptical of any company that will not give its name, address, phone number, and references.

- Thoroughly check out any company that you are thinking of doing business with at the Better Business Bureau, the State Attorney General's Office, or your local consumer protection agency.
- Report fraud to your local Better Business Bureau and to state and local law enforcement agencies.
- The areas in which fraudulent sales are most often attempted when concerning seniors are: medical and health; house, roof, and driveway repairs; tree and yard services; investment clubs; and vacation homes.

Fraud

13.1 OVERVIEW

The deception begins when you answer the telephone and a slick salesman on the other line says you have won a vacation. Sooner or later, everyone is approached by a con artist. Con artists are smart, persuasive, and aggressive. Your best defense is to use common sense. Anything that sounds too good to be true probably is.

In general, be suspicious of any solicitation for home repairs, insurance, or investments that seem to offer something for nothing. Do business with established companies that have good reputations. Never provide anyone with cash unless you have an enforceable guarantee.

13.2 TELEPHONE

Telephones are easy ways for con artists to sell or promote bogus services or products, including all types of investments, donations, and vacation property. If you have any suspicions about a company that is doing business over the telephone, contact the Better Business Bureau, your State Attorney General's Office, or your local consumer protection agency.

If you believe that you have been a victim of telephone fraud, contact your State Attorney General's Office for information about prosecuting the company. Remember these tips to avoid telephone fraud:

- Do not give your credit card numbers, Social Security number, or checking account information over the telephone unless you know exactly who you are dealing with.
- Make sure you know the charges before calling a 900 number. While 800 numbers and 888 numbers are free, 900 numbers are not.
- Request a financial report if a caller requests a donation from a charity with which you are not familiar.
- Be skeptical of any company that will not give its name, address, telephone number, and references.
- Never make an investment with a stranger over the telephone.
- Be suspicious of anyone calling from the telephone company or a law enforcement agency who asks for your telephone card number.
- Report lost or stolen calling cards immediately.
- Never accept a collect call or a third party call if you are not certain who is making the call.
- Be careful at airports, hotels, and public pay telephones.
- Cover the keypad when you enter your access codes and PINs.
- Speak quietly when placing operator-assisted calls.
- Be aware of people loitering around pay telephones. They may be attempting to steal access codes and PINs.
- Watch your monthly reports and telephone bills for mistakes and calls you did not make.
- Report suspicious activity, such as repetitive hang-up calls or frequent wrong numbers.
- If you use a cellular telephone, keep it out of sight when not in use. Report a lost or stolen telephone immediately.

13.3 MAIL

Like most companies that sell products over the telephone, most mail order firms are honest and stand behind their products or services. But many con artists use the mail to sell you worthless merchandise and get-rich-quick schemes. Here are some tips to reduce your risk of being a victim of mail fraud:

- Watch out for letters or postcards that say you can win something by calling a 900 number.

- Some scams begin when you are sent merchandise that you never ordered. You do not have to pay for this merchandise.

If you think you have been cheated in a mail fraud scheme, keep all the letters and envelopes and contact the US Postal Service or the Attorney General's Office in your state.

13.4 INVESTMENT SCHEMES

Investment schemes are often presented with an appeal or sales pitch that sounds too good to be true, such as the following:

- "Here is a no-risk investment."
- "You have won! We just need to take out the taxes."
- "We need to verify your credit rating and account number before we can provide this special information."
- "It is easy to make money. There will only be a one-time charge to your account."

Other glowing and unbelievable testimonials are often used to convince you that you can make a great deal of money without effort and work. If it sounds too good to be true, it probably is.

13.5 CREDIT CARDS AND CHECKING ACCOUNTS

The key to your credit cards and checking accounts are your account numbers. High-tech thieves attempt to get these numbers in one form or another, since that may be all that they need to illegally charge items to your account or draw funds from it.

- Never give your checking account number over the telephone. Use a credit card, and provide the number only when you have initiated a call to make a purchase.
- A telemarketing or direct mail approach is often used to get your checking account number under the guise of selling a product or service. Once the number is obtained, false demand drafts can be submitted to your account.
- Use only one or two credit cards and keep a close watch on your credit card statements. If you notice anything unexpected, call the credit card company immediately.

13.6 MEDICAL

Some con artists take advantage of everyone's desire for better health and good looks. Quacks and self-proclaimed health care experts promise quick cures for anything from cancer and diabetes to obesity and hair loss. Some of these remedies can have dangerous side-effects and can prevent people from getting proper medical treatment. Be especially wary of

- exaggerated claims, testimonials, and secret ingredients;
- attacks on traditional medicine or nutrition;
- promises of quick cures; or
- someone demanding cash for a purchase.

Seniors and elderly people tend to be more vulnerable to medical- and health-related fraud. If you have a parent or an elderly friend who seems to be interested in a medical or health-related program that promises more than is normally reasonable, take some time to help them examine all the claims and fine print. If you have concerns about the program's legitimacy, call your State Attorney General's Office for a background check on the promoter.

13.7 STOLEN IDENTITY

Although recent amendments to the Fair Credit Reporting Act make it easier for consumers to correct mistakes in their credit reports, these amendments will not stop the growth of a particularly damaging credit problem: Identity theft. For individual consumers, the best way to protect against identity theft is to zealously guard one's personal credit information.

If you are rejected for employment or other applications based upon a background investigation, it may have been caused by someone who has used your identity for a variety of illegitimate reasons. Traditionally, consumer credit fraud involves thieves stealing credit cards or checks. Victims usually have to deal with only one creditor or a few forged checks to resolve the situation.

Identity theft, also called "account takeover" or "true name" fraud, presents victims with problems more difficult and more time consuming to correct. Thieves can obtain someone's personal information in various ways, but increasingly detailed personal information is available from public and private electronic databases and can be stolen by computer. After obtaining Social Security numbers, birth dates, driver's license numbers, or other identifiers, thieves may use this personal information to commit the following frauds:

- Obtain false identification
- Take over existing credit and bank accounts
- Open new accounts
- Take out loans
- Pass bogus checks
- Steal cash, goods, and services

According to the US Department of Justice, "the Bureau of Justice Statistics estimates of the annual financial loss caused by identity theft are on the order of $17.3 billion in 2007 and 2008."[1] Most fraud losses are absorbed by creditors, but victims of identity theft usually face a series of problems as they try to resolve the situation, including the need to contact many creditors and agencies.

The US Public Interest Research Group, with help from the Privacy Rights Clearinghouse of California, suggests that consumers take the following steps when they realize they are victims of identity theft.

13.7.1 Credit Bureaus
Call the fraud units of the three major credit reporting bureaus (Equifax: (800) 525–6285; Experian: (800) 301–7195; and TransUnion: (800) 680–7289). Follow up with letters to their mailing addresses. Have your credit reports flagged to prevent future fraudulent accounts.

13.7.2 Check Verification Companies
If a thief uses your identity to cash a bad check, someone will soon refuse your check. In addition to contacting your bank to set up a new checking account, contact one or several of the six major check verification companies to clear your name (Chexsystems: (800) 428–9623; Equifax: (800) 437–5120; TeleCheck: (800) 710–9898; National Processing Co.: (800) 526–5380; CheckRite: (800) 766–2748; and SCAN: (800) 262–7771).

---

[1]Rod J. Rosenstein, and Tamera Fine, "Identity Theft: Coordination Can Defeat the Modern-Day 'King' and 'Duke'," US Department of Justice, accessed September 19, 2013, http://www.justice.gov/usao/briefing_room/fin/id_theft.html.

13.7.3 Creditors

Immediately contact all creditors with whom your name has been used fraudulently. Obtain replacement cards with new numbers for all related accounts. Ask that the old accounts be processed as "account closed at consumer's request."

13.7.4 ATM Cards

If your ATM card has been stolen or compromised, obtain a new card, account number, and password. When creating a new password, do not use common numbers like the last four digits of your Social Security number or your birth date.

13.7.5 Change of Address

Call the local postal inspector if you suspect an identity thief has filed a fraudulent change of address order to get your mail and personal information.

13.7.6 Social Security Number

Your Social Security number is the key to most electronic databases. Call the Social Security Administration at (800) 772–1213 to report fraudulent use of your number. In some cases, if you meet Social Security fraud criteria, you may receive a replacement number.

13.7.7 Driver's License Number

You may need to change your driver's license number if someone is using yours as identification on bad checks. Call your state's registry of motor vehicles for further details.

13.7.8 Telephone Service

If your long distance calling card is stolen, or you discover fraudulent charges on your bill, report this to the carrier and open a new account. Also look out for utility bills opened by thieves using your Social Security number.

13.7.9 Affidavits

You may be asked by creditors to provide notarized affidavits supporting your report of identity theft. The law does not require that such affidavits be notarized, but you may want to provide them if requested for your own protection.

CHAPTER 14

Personal Security Resources

This chapter provides lists of resources available at local and national organizations. The organizations listed here can supply advice and information, as well as help you find additional resources that may be useful in your particular situation. The National Crime Prevention Council is a good resource for help in many areas relating to personal security.

National Crime Prevention Council
2345 Crystal Drive
Suite 500
Arlington, VA 22202
http://www.ncpc.org/
(202) 466–6272

14.1 LOCAL RESOURCES

In every community, there are a number of local resources you can draw on for personal security assistance. Search the Web and local registries for accident, crime, and emergency prevention and preparedness offices. If you need assistance finding local resources, contact one or all of the following:

- Local, provincial, state, regional, national, or global governmental or non-governmental (NGOs) safety offices
- Accident, crime, and fire prevention, or disaster preparedness agencies
- Social services departments
- Board of Education

14.2 ALL-HAZARDS PREPAREDNESS

- Centers for Disease Control and Prevention (http://www.bt.cdc.gov/hazards-all.asp)
- Federal Emergency Management Agency (FEMA) (http://www.fema.gov/)
- Are You Ready? (http://www.fema.gov/pdf/areyouready/areyouready_full.pdf)
- The US Fire Administration Library (http://www.usfa.fema.gov/library/)
- National Safety Council http://www.nsc.org/safety_home/Pages/safety_at_hom.aspx

14.3 CHILDREN

- National Center for Missing and Exploited Children
  http://www.missingkids.com/home
  24-hour call center: 1-800-THE-LOST (1-800-843-5678)
- National Runaway Safeline
  http://www.1800runaway.org/
  (800) RUNAWAY (800-786-2929)
- National School Safety Center
  http://www.schoolsafety.us/
  (805) 373–9977
- The Center on Addiction and the Family
  http://www.phoenixhouse.org/family/center-on-addiction-and-the-family/
  (888) 286–5027
- The World Health Organization
  http://www.who.int/violence_injury_prevention/child/en/

14.4 DRUGS AND ALCOHOL

- Alcoholics Anonymous
  http://www.aa.org/
  Helpline: (866)783–7712
- American Council on Alcoholism
  http://www.aca-usa.org/
- Center on Addiction and the Family
  http://www.coaf.org/
  (888) 286–5027

- Cocaine Anonymous
  http://www.ca.org/
- Marijuana Anonymous
  http://www.marijuana-anonymous.org/
- Narcotics Anonymous
  http://www.na.org/
- National Council on Alcoholism and Drug Dependence
  http://www.addictionsearch.com/addiction-treatment/AZ-8841/
  national-council-on-alcoholism-drug-dependence/
  (800) 559–9503
- Substance Abuse and Mental Health Services Administration
  (SAMHSA)
  http://www.samhsa.gov/
  National Helpline (also known as the Treatment Referral Routing
  Service): (800) 662-HELP (4357)
  Disaster Distress Helpline: (800) 985–5990
- National Suicide Prevention Lifeline
  http://www.suicidepreventionlifeline.org/
  (800) 273-TALK (8255)
- Drug Enforcement Administration, US Department of Justice
  http://www.usdoj.gov/dea/index.htm
  (202) 307–1000

14.5 PREVENTING BIAS-MOTIVATED VIOLENCE

- American-Arab Anti-Discrimination Committee
  http://www.adc.org/
- Anti-Defamation League
  http://www.adl.org/
- Community Relations Service, US Department of Justice
  http://www.usdoj.gov/crs/
- Japanese American Citizens League
  http://www.jacl.org/
- The National Conference for Community and Justice (NCCJ)
  http://www.nccj.org/
- National Gay and Lesbian Task Force
  http://www.thetaskforce.org/
- Organization of Chinese Americans
  http://www.ocanational.org/

- Southern Poverty Law Center
  http://www.splcenter.org/intel/intpro.jsp

14.6 VICTIM ASSISTANCE

14.6.1 Crimes and Crises
- National Organization for Victim Assistance
  http://www.trynova.org/
- National Center for Victims of Crime
  http://www.victimsofcrime.org/
- Operation Identification
  http://www.opid.org/
- Office for Victims of Crime, US Department of Justice
  http://www.ojp.usdoj.gov/ovc/

14.6.2 Disasters
- Federal Emergency Management Agency (FEMA) Disaster Survivor Assistance
  http://www.fema.gov/disaster-survivor-assistance
- International Federation of Red Cross and Red Crescent Societies
  http://www.ifrc.org/

About the Contributing Editor

Francis is a principal of Crime Prevention Associates and emeritus faculty of the Security Executive Council. He is a Certified Protection Professional (CPP), Fraud Examiner (CFE), Community Emergency Responder, Food Defense Coordinator, and Coffee Master.

He is a seasoned all-hazards risk mitigation leader for multinational convenience, food and beverage, manufacturing, restaurant, retail, and supply chain operators. He has served as chief security officer for Starbucks Coffee, Hardees Food Systems, and Jerrico Inc. His expertise includes risk diligence, loss prevention and mitigation systems design, as well as contribution analytics.

Francis was named one of the "25 Most Influential People in Security" in 2009 by *Security* magazine, and was a *CSO* magazine 2007 Compass Award honoree.

He is also the critically acclaimed author of *The Manager's Violence Survival Guide* (1995), *Loss Prevention through Crime Analysis* (1989), and *Influencing Enterprise Risk Mitigation* (2013).

About Elsevier's Security Executive Council Risk Management Portfolio

Elsevier's Security Executive Council Risk Management Portfolio is the voice of the security leader. It equips executives, practitioners, and educators with research-based, proven information and practical solutions for successful security and risk management programs. This portfolio covers topics in the areas of risk mitigation and assessment, ideation and implementation, and professional development. It brings trusted operational research, risk management advice, tactics, and tools to business professionals. Previously available only to the Security Executive Council community, this content—covering corporate security, enterprise crisis management, global IT security, and more—provides real-world solutions and "how-to" applications.

The Security Executive Council (www.securityexecutivecouncil.com) is a leading problem-solving research and services organization focused on helping businesses build value while improving their ability to effectively manage and mitigate risk. Drawing on the collective knowledge of a large community of successful security practitioners, experts, and strategic alliance partners, the Council develops strategy and insight and identifies proven practices that cannot be found anywhere else. Their research, services, and tools are focused on protecting people, brand, information, physical assets, and the bottom line.

Elsevier (www.elsevier.com) is an international multimedia publishing company that provides world-class information and innovative solutions tools. It is part of Reed Elsevier, a world-leading provider of professional information solutions in the science, medical, risk, legal, and business sectors.

Printed and bound by CPI Group (UK) Ltd, Croydon, CR0 4YY

08/05/2025

01864891-0001